Hero's Highway

Pray for our heroes

Hero's Highway

A Chaplain's Journey Toward Forgiveness Inside A Combat Hospital

Norris Burkes

Chaplain Norris Burkes

ISBN: 0692397000
ISBN 13: 9780692397008

This book is dedicated to the 332d Expeditionary Medical Group in Balad Iraq – proud military descendants of the Tuskegee Airmen.

CONTENTS

PREFACE

In January of 2009, I began a four-month deployment as the senior hospital chaplain at the Air Force Field Hospital in Balad, Iraq. On the day I arrived, I was told that our hospital trauma room had recently become the busiest in the world, treating over 1000 patients a month. Many of those patients arrived by helicopter, were placed on gurneys, and rolled through the ambulance bay into our emergency room.

Covering that bay was a fabric tent structure resembling a carport. The soldiers on those gurneys looked up to see the large American flag covering the ceiling of the bay. When they heard the medical staff greet them with the words, "Welcome to Hero's Highway," they knew their chances of survival were better than 97%.

This book is dedicated to the heroes I met on that highway. While their names are fictionalized for the purposes of this book, they remain true-life heroes.

ABOUT THIS AUTHOR

Burkes recently retired from the California Air National Guard without ever quite achieving his grandiose goal of becoming a four-star general. He currently serves as a hospital chaplain in Northern California. He is certified by the Association of Professional Chaplains, which is mostly different from being "certifiable."

Burkes graduated from Baylor University, Waco, TX with a Bachelor of Arts in religion and journalism. He received a Master's of Divinity from Golden Gate Seminary and a Master's of Fine Arts in *Creative Nonfiction* from Pacific University. (Note the emphasis on "creative nonfiction.")

In recent years, he has run two marathons, completing his last marathon in a little over 5 hours. Last year, he took up golf, but doesn't claim he can be trusted with keeping accurate score.

He is also the author of No Small Miracles, the father of four grown miracles and living proof that 35 plus-years of a happy marriage is still God's greatest miracle. He plans to write more books and go to cooking school, but his wife doesn't believe him.

Contact him at ask@thechaplain.net or P.O. Box 247, Elk Grove, CA 95759. Twitter @chaplain. Leave your recorded comments at (843) 608-9715. Read more at www.thechaplain.net.

ACKNOWLEDGEMENTS

First, I want to thank my many proofreaders – Becky Burkes, Petra Stanton, Davalynn Spencer, Jennifer Stevens, and Roger Williams. I also owe a great deal to the staff, advisors, and students at the MFA program at Pacific University. While way too many to mention, special shout-outs go to Debra Gwartney, Elinor Langer, Mike Magnuson, and Tiffany Hauck.

Finally, my biggest gratitude goes to the approximately 357 professional members of 332d Expeditionary Medical Group in Balad Iraq. A proud descendent of the Tuskegee Airmen, they provided a full-spectrum of heroic medical services for Coalition and U.S. forces throughout the Iraqi theater of operations. It was inactivated on 8 May 2012.

CHAPTER 1

THE REASON I GO

Why would anyone want to volunteer to serve in a combat zone? This was the unanswerable question my friends and family were asking me in the fall of 2008. I couldn't easily articulate the answer, but if I could have shown them the answer, I'd have pointed to the grieving faces of mothers and fathers, wives or husbands, sons and daughters. These were the faces I met behind two dozen doors I knocked upon to bring the unimaginable news of a loved one lost to war.

I encountered families in all kinds of situations and places. I met them inside manicured subdivisions and camper shells. I stopped them in their driveways as they left for work and in their garages working under their cars. I interrupted their dinners, birthday parties, and their family fights. I met their small children, their big dogs, and their nosey neighbors.

They reacted in a variety of ways. They froze in disbelief or exploded in disbelief. They fainted in shock or erupted with profanity. They insisted we were mistaken or they asked when they could expect the life insurance money. They even offered us tea and cookies.

For me, notifications always began with a phone call from the California National Guard Headquarters:

"Major Burkes." I recognized the baritone voice of Staff Sergeant Desmond Knight. "We need you to accompany a Military Casualty Affairs Officer for another death notification."

And wherever I was – in a parent/teacher conference for one of my four children, or in my civilian role as a hospital chaplain baptizing a premature baby, or in a romantic moment with my wife – I'd rush to my walk-in closet and emerge wearing a blue service coat with colored ribbons stacked nearly to my Adam's apple, dark blue trousers, a light blue long-sleeved shirt, a herringbone tie, and black plain-tipped shoes. After putting on my hat, I'd leave the house to meet a Sergeant I didn't know, and we'd go to a town I couldn't pronounce to deliver the news no one could imagine.

It happened too many times, and each time I saw Sgt. Knight's name on my caller ID, I wanted to hang up. When I did answer, I offered excuses. If the excuses weren't accepted, I shed my minister role and assumed the safer mode of messenger. Once inside the homes, I looked at my watch and asked disinterested questions. I came home angry about the slightest things and found sleep illusive. When I shared these symptoms with a colleague in military mental health, she offered to write a note excusing me from notification duty for one year due to mental anguish. I refused her offer because it felt like the families had paid a much bigger cost than I. Who was I to claim mental anguish?

It took Number 25 to get my attention. That was the summer day in 2007 when I went to Napa, California, to tell a mother that she had lost her only son. I made the trip with Sergeant Alicia Gutierrez, an army non-commissioned officer in her mid-thirties. This was her first notification, and she brought a black binder full of notes and a heart without guile. Her army dress uniform tugged at her chest, and her blonde hair formed a crowning bun. A chin scar told me she'd once connected with something extremely hard, but it was the accompanying hash marks on her sleeve and her mountain of pocket accouterments that told me of her experience.

She drove our beige government sedan along the snaking Napa Valley. Fields of tall summer grass bent in the crystal sunshine like an old man's whiskers blowing in the wind while sunflowers and lupine joined the parade of lush purple grapes stretching through the everlasting valley. Limos passed us ferrying dot-com millionaires on weekend getaways between wineries, and tourists floated above us in what brochures described as the "iconic Napa Valley ballooning experience."

We drove past bird watchers who came to Napa to worship in their ornithological temple. They congregated on nearby fire roads to survey the bufflehead and osprey that migrated to nearby Lake Hennessey to spread the rumor that it was possible to go home again. The valley was alive with the chatter and flutter of sparrows working to disprove what Jesus said: "Look at the sparrows of the field, they neither toil nor spin." If the birdwatchers had known our mission, they may have realized that they were the ones being observed. Perhaps they were just the minor entertainment of a voyeuristic god who categorized each of them by species and sex.

But none of it seemed genuine that day. The birds, limos, wine tasters, and balloons were all part of a naïve daydream buried in a nightmare. Gutierrez and I were carrying truth like smugglers with foreign contraband. We were going to tell Mrs. Louise Addison that her son, Private First Class Steven Addison, was dead.

During the drive, I started wondering how Number 25 would compare to notifications I'd made with other teams. Perhaps we would meet another anguished father who would launch into a political diatribe blaming President Bush for his son's death. It was even possible we would interrupt another fun-night for a couple returning from midnight bingo. I only hoped it wouldn't repeat the Christmas Eve morning when we interrupted a family's airport reunion to tell them their son wasn't on the plane, or that it wouldn't be like the day we disrupted a child's birthday party. Mostly, I was worried that the family would discover I had never been to battle and they would say, "You can't know what it means to see someone die."

I wasn't sure what Gutierrez was thinking until she steered our sedan onto a gravel turnout within a half-mile of the unsuspecting home. She skidded to a stop and jerked the gearshift into park and abruptly spoke to her driver's side window.

"Chaplain, would you say a prayer for us?"

"Yes," I said. "I can do that." I heard my own doubts in the promise. Was she asking if I would or was she asking if I could? I didn't have many prayers remaining. The shelf life of the prayers I'd once used to thank God for "those who died defending our freedom" had long since expired, as had the justification to begin our war. The logistics of integrity proved a tricky thing.

But, yes, I could enunciate a prayer, so I did. I said the words, hoping not to lose myself in a memorized maze of banalities. If I had been straightforward, my supplication would have sounded more like a curse than a prayer. It would have been the one I pounded into my car's steering wheel before leaving home: "God, not again!" But I doubt if Gutierrez would have been thankful for such lucidity, so I offered her my hand and began a prayer of abbreviated sincerity.

"God, we're scared." She squeezed my hand with a familiar emptiness. "We don't know how to bring this news, but we do know that we'll need your help. Amen." She retracted her hand and dabbed at her streaking mascara and pinged me a searching expression for more.

"Stick to the plan," I answered. "It's all I know to do." Nothing about the unannounced visits was ever in our control. So yes, the prayer helped, but yes, that's all there was.

A few minutes later, we found an address that didn't want to be found in a three-home cul-de-sac gouged into a steep, forested hill. We parked on the hillside and walked past two porches where neighborhood sentries dared our entourage to breach the boundaries drawn by late afternoon shadows. A creek gurgled its way through the property while chortling bluebirds seemed convinced that it should be an ordinary day.

The home materialized as the last of three in a forest clearing. With its bay windows, it looked much like the proverbial glass house where secrets found no quarter. We approached the door and paused on the dirt porch, juggling our reluctance with our clipboards and hats. We gave the old growth redwood door a knock that started the crack in the mother's glass world.

The door swung wide revealing a petite 5-foot-something woman dressed in a corporate suit. Her pursed lips and rounded nose were blocked tightly inside the margin of a curly crop of brown hair. She cocked her thin, graying eyes and took aim at our uniforms as if trying to repel unwanted news. But our opening question discharged the unspeakable, and it was too late to turn us around.

"Are you Mrs. Louise Addison?" asked Gutierrez.

She gave a hesitant nod as if stalling to produce an optional identity.

"Ma'am," Staff Sergeant Gutierrez asked. "May we come in?"

"Why? What's this all about?" Lies come in questions, too. I repeated our request.

"No!" she said. Her eyes refocused on my chaplain's cross. "Not if ...." She reset her jaw and formed a clairvoyant prediction. "Not if you are going to tell me my son's dead!"

We answered by taking a nervous interest in our shoe polish.

"Oh, my God. No!" she screamed. She dropped to her knees, folding into the ground like a falling tree and staining her pleated slacks with a varnish of tree mulch and mud.

"Oh my God, he's dead, and it's my fault," she said.

We reached for her, one of us on each arm, but she wanted to remain planted.

"I'm sorry, so sorry, ma'am," Gutierrez said. I echoed the sentiment, but Mrs. Addison resisted our tired formulas, pulling at her ears and hair as if somehow trying to extract her new reality. Her tears moved into wailing and her wailing became an endless babble of blame and pain. We stooped down to encourage her to stand, but she slung her arms away, refusing us a hold. Finally, her wailing summoned a blue-haired neighbor woman who approached us like we had just assaulted her neighbor. She was right. We had.

The woman was smaller than Mrs. Addison, but her companion gave her the strength needed to walk inside and take a seat on a leather couch. Sergeant Gutierrez unfolded the script from her coat pocket while I took in a living room of family pictures sitting like dominoes on the fireplace mantle and upright piano. The room was walled by picture windows that seduced my thoughts into the surrounding forest.

Gutierrez cleared her throat and Mrs. Addison shook her head like she was facing a firing squad. Gutierrez fired: "The Secretary of the Army has asked me to express his deep regret that your son, Private First Class Steven Addison, was killed by an improvised explosive device while riding in his Humvee five miles outside of Camp Victory, Iraq. The Secretary extends his deepest sympathy to you and your family in your tragic loss."

The notification script was one peppered with a measured accuracy, and we only said what we precisely knew to be true and nothing more. Nevertheless, it came from Gutierrez like an explosive projectile.

"No! God, no! Please, God, no!"

This time Mrs. Addison screams made me feel like we were floating in a place where truth and anger come together like the currents of Cape Horn meeting opposing winds. Her sobs became whitecap waves that eroded her face with scars of self-reproach. The next few minutes stretched around the globe, but when her shoulders finally softened, she squeezed out a sobbing question. "What happened? Why? Why? Why?" She wasn't asking because of her failure to hear or because she didn't know. She was asking what I'd been asking since doing so many notifications.

Grief can light up the soul in a thunderous flashpoint of desolation and wretchedness. We watched the news propagate, infect, and ultimately replicate into a thousand shattered forms. The tears receded, and we began our routine exit of memorized questions. "Would you like me to say a prayer? Do you have other family or friends you can call? Do you have a pastor, doctor or counselor?" We were grateful she had friends and family because we didn't need the exclusive on this notification. We were surrogate support and we were willing to franchise the grief among the genuineness of real friends. Phone calls would be made; grief would expand exponentially and then go viral.

"Are there any more questions for us?" asked the sergeant.

"No," Addison said.

Right answer. We exchanged hugs like business cards and left her with a new identity, one without a name. There is a title for a person who loses a spouse – "widow" or "widower." A child without parents is an orphan. But what do you call a parent who has lost a child?

Gutierrez and I made a stealthy retreat through the shroud of grief and returned to our picturesque day. On the drive home, I settled into the passenger seat and searched for hawks on the passing fence posts. The surrounding hills reminded me of the San Francisco Bay Area where I played war as a child. My friends and I would often choose our combat cadre based on the shared armament available. In our unkempt thrift-store coats, we'd bring a hodgepodge of squirt guns, cap guns, stick guns, and if all else failed, a clicking thumb atop a shuddering index finger. We'd play until suppertime or until the rain started or until the youngest squealed to his mommy that we were playing too rough.

Most of us kids wanted to be on the side with Ronald Landers or his brother Dennis, but no one wanted to play against them because everyone knew that the Landers boys cheated. Whether we played with plastic army men spread along the side of the sandbox or faced off the brothers in a cap gun fight, they'd cheat. With their slick-backed hair and choose-me grins, they'd melt certainty into doubt and forge words into excuses. Whenever I "shot" one of them, he'd say that I missed or even counterclaim that I had been killed in the crossfire. The brothers were convincing, so I had to be dead for a while. It was always the same; whenever we shot them, they wouldn't be dead. They'd make up stupid excuses like how they were wearing bulletproof vests or something.

Maybe that's what inspired me to use chalky sheetrock pieces to write "Dennis Landers is a ratfink" on the brown shack that housed our neighborhood trashcans. I wrote those words believing that he shouldn't have been allowed to come back from the dead unless he had waited the appropriate amount of dead time. When you shoot somebody, they are supposed to stay down until the war is won, and then they can get up and play again. You stick to the script you get. Those were the rules. Death must follow rules.

I briefly wondered what rules Addison's death followed. I wondered what it might be like to see where Addison died and what really killed him, but the passing fence posts made me feel vertiginous and I closed my eyes.

Gutierrez was silent, so I started humming a random tune to fill the discomfort of quiet. "The sun'll come out tomorrow. Bet your bottom dollar that tomorrow. There'll be sun."

Gutierrez kept driving and I went back to staring out the window while I tried to convince myself with childhood logic that there would be sun tomorrow and that Addison would get up and play again.

When the sun made its regularly scheduled appearance the next morning, I took my pound-pup Chewy on a jog along the creekside trail that intersects my orderly Sacramento subdivision. I tried not to think about Addison, but notifications like that always brought back the first one I did, 20 years earlier on January 17, 1989. It started when I heard radio reports of a man shooting scores of students with a semi-automatic assault rifle at Cleveland Elementary School. Sixty minutes after hearing the report, I drove to the school and introduced myself to the on-scene commander as an Air Force Reserve chaplain with training in trauma pastoral care. He paused to study my 32-year-old face and then sent me into a room where parents and counselors were waiting for a list of casualties and hospital admissions. The unspoken truth was that we weren't waiting on a list of survivors: we were waiting on confirmation of the dead.

Thirty minutes later an officer nudged the classroom door open and handed me the fatality list. He whispered his instructions and pointed me toward a Cambodian mother and her eleven-year-old son. The boy was leaning into his mother's lap in the same way I'd leaned into my own mother's lap while we sat on a church pew. They were holding – no, squeezing – each other's hands and holding a tissue. She didn't speak English, but I think she understood that the room was a ruse. Without an interpreter for the mother, I had few options but to simply place my finger on her daughter's listed name and shake my head. I didn't need words. What the hell would words have done anyway? My clinical training taught me that these are the moments a chaplain can provide dignity to death, but at that moment, all I wanted to do was to run from the room in the most undignified manner.

The woman recognized her daughter's name and asked, "Sh-di?" I did not understand her. Our eyes collided with a pained look of confusion.

"Sh-di?" she repeated.

Squinting to convey my confusion, suddenly I understood.

I didn't need an interpreter. "Sh-di?" meant, "Did she die?"

"Yes," I said looking into the woman's sunbaked face.

Her eyes swept the room searching for a second opinion but received only a nod from her son to confirm the translation. I wanted to cry, but this instinct seemed counterfeit. I did not understand her grief. Why would I need to cry, too? Neither she nor her son even moved. She did not cry. But suddenly, in something that can only be described as emotional ventriloquism, her grief began to squeeze through her son's eyes, and a tear furrowed down his face. He was her emotional surrogate shedding the tears her culture forbade her to produce.

The memory of the Cambodian family ends there. I spent two more days on the scene talking to the staff before becoming overwhelmed with the paralyzing realization of how easily this could have been my daughter's class. When school district administrators asked for volunteers to return the following week, I took the truant approach and never returned. I had assumed that I'd be able to turn my pain inside out like a stained sweatshirt made ready to wear again. I was wrong. Twenty years later, as I walked along our subdivision's trail, I was still wearing my stained sweatshirt.

A worn path cut through the leafy creek bed and offered a shortcut back into streets of cloned houses competing for architectural legitimacy. Soon I saw a familiar whiteboard sign affixed to 5611 Sierra Drive. Its daily missive gave the weekly tally of distasteful digits:

War Dead: Afghanistan 1248. Iraq 4417.

This time was different, though. This time the resident was outside making her way around the edge of her artistic lawn with a watering hose. She was a bent elderly woman who had likely lived through a few wars, maybe even waged a few herself.

"Howdy," I said.

Without turning, she kept watering her plants.

I yelled a bit louder. "Howdy!"

"Hello." She finally said.

"What's the story on your whiteboard?" I asked. "Do you know someone who died in the war?"

"We all have someone who has died over there," she said and turned her watering hose on her hibiscus before adding a well-timed punch line. "They were all Americans, and we should consider each of them a part of our family."

"Good point," I said. I felt breathless from both my jog and her memorized homily.

"Do you ever get any complaints?" I asked.

"The numbers have been erased a few times," she admitted. "Most people just walk past. Besides, what would they complain about? It's accurate!" She pointed to the sign's subtext she'd coined to dismiss magical thinking: "Erasing the numbers doesn't erase their deaths."

"Guess not," I agreed and said my goodbyes. I did not mention the 25 names I'd like to erase.

I jogged into an adjoining park and benched myself with grief as if I were an injured athlete. I folded over, gripping my calves, trying to stifle my desire to cry for all those names. I didn't know how to cry for that many people even if I could. Of course Jesus knew. He cried for them on a mountaintop outside of Jerusalem and resumed his tears while hanging from a cross. Mother Theresa knew how to cry as she did her tearful penitence in the Calcutta slums, but I had little qualification to shed the tears of the innocent. I could have cried for the discounted and the uncounted, but I didn't know how many Iraqi soldiers lay buried in sand ditches. I didn't know how many children had become the collateral damage of roadside bombs. I couldn't quantify the humiliation of the Abu Ghraib prisoners or measure the terror of the waterboarding victims.

Yet among all the incalculable sums, there was one number I did know: zero. Zero was the amount of times I'd been to war. Zero was the amount of personal risk I'd endured. Zero was what I knew about the sacrifices men made in war. I pulled myself from my bench, and even as I walked home, I knew that I would go to Iraq for these answers. To the 24 + 1, I promised I would go.

When I got home, I found a blinking answering machine light and pushed the play button. "Chaplain Burkes," asked the voice of a local funeral director. "Are you available to officiate the funeral of Private First Class Steven Addison?"

Two days later, I found my way into the half-circle driveway of a funeral home in the heart of a town begging to be memorialized by a Thomas Kinkade painting. I parked in the clergy space and took the stepping-stone path through the chapel garden where I met the voice from the answering machine.

"Beautiful day!" the funeral director reported. It was beautiful. It wasn't yet eleven and apparently the song I'd been humming on the drive home from the death notification had correctly predicted at least a week of hot weather.

"Yes, it is," I said.

"I'm Jim Davis, owner," he said. His new suit flared my cynicism. I knew how much money the government threw at funerals and was sure that his wallet was having a beautiful day. He pointed toward the line of police cars blocking the adjoining street. "Lots of folks coming," he said. There weren't just lots of folks, there were all kinds of folks using the rows of canopied trees as a shelter from the predicted of 102 degrees. There were young women in miniskirts and old women pushing walkers. There were children dressed like they were going to Sunday school and young men tattooed like they'd been to war. Most every one of them were wearing sunglasses. Women perched them atop swirling hairdos, and men wore them backwards on their heads.

I suppose they figured they needed the glasses to hide the tears they promised to never shed. They needed them to either conceal their tears or flush their tears. There was no middle ground. Mourners are afraid their tears will become unpredictable, uncontrollable or unstoppable. Funeral tears can quickly unravel people. I was at the funeral to orchestrate emotion that should be neither too tightly held nor too laxly dispersed. Crying still seemed like such a useless activity, but was is all we knew to do.

At 11 sharp, I took my place inside the chapel and stood at the podium with a limp prayer clogging my throat like a glob of expectorant. While handkerchiefs were being charged with heartache, my abrupt cough expelled the prayer that started the memorial. "God, help us to honor Steven in a celebration of his life." My words came out sounding like I was daring God to help us see significance in Steven's sacrifice.

After my plea, three friends dutifully reminisced their partying days and their carefree nights with Steven. They made speeches about God and girlfriends, football and fights, dinners and dives. They testified that he was their best friend, and by-god, they would never forget him.

After their speeches, a two-star general and Texas import stood to corroborate the honor of a soldier he never met. With perfunctory adulation and verbosity he reported that yes, Addison was a good soldier and, yes, a brave warrior. He turned to the casket and presented a final salute and laid two posthumous medals on the polished redwood. Then he cued me to lead the military pallbearers outside to the waiting hearse where a leather-vested group of Vietnam Veterans sat atop parked Harleys.

"Mount up!" shouted their over-stuffed tattooed leader. His command launched a two-mile motorcade of headlights in search of significance against the noonday sun.

We drove though the heart of the red-bricked town where hundreds of people held hands over their hearts trying to clot a hemorrhage of heartache. The church bells rang for Steven and mimicked the sound of a soul struggling to be someone other than who he had become. On the sidewalks, police officers, aging veterans, and Boy Scout troops charged the crowd with patriotic salutes. Fire trucks blockaded the side streets with the hometown pageantry of blinking lights and siren blips.

I soon realized that these were the crossroads where Steven had lived his life. I imagined his childhood days when his third-grade class visited the fire station and emerged wearing fireman hats that swallowed their cherubic faces. Nearby, a candy cane pole marked the old town barbershop where he got perhaps his first haircut and then his last haircut before entering basic training. At the edge of town, we passed his high school football field and I considered whether he joined the military to find the prestige that eluded him on the gridiron.

At the dead-end of this aimlessly rural road, a snapping flag affixed atop a towering crane beckoned us into the cemetery driveway. The hearse stopped and soldiers slid the casket from its hold, thereby fulfilling their promise never to leave a comrade behind, even on the battlefield of their mind. I led the pallbearers in a slow dance of measured steps over the grave markers that shared their testimony from the famed poem, Flanders Field:

We are the Dead. Short days ago
We lived, felt dawn, saw sunset glow,
Loved and were loved, and now we lie
In Flanders fields.

Our parade paused near a canvas-sheltered gravesite and the pallbearers looked toward me for direction. I gave them an assenting bow, and they laid the casket on the canvas slats of a ratcheted platform crane perched over a freshly dug grave. The funeral director motioned me to begin my short day-end reprise. I read a passage from *The Problem of Pain*, by C.S. Lewis, in which Lewis says that God doesn't cause tragedies but rather uses them to speak to us. The book, which has always inspired me, had a hollow ring that day, but it was all I knew to read.

I opened my Bible to the routine passage of the 23rd Psalm, "Though I walk through the valley of the shadow of death. Thou art with me." I looked to my side, hoping "Thou" was there.

"And I shall dwell in the house of the Lord forever. Amen." Why forever? Now would be a better time, because forever is, well, a long time from now. Besides, I wondered if "forever" could possibly be long enough. I dropped my chin and said the benedictory prayer. It was all I knew to do.

My "amen" cued a noncommissioned officer to position his three-man firing detail. They aimed their rifles toward the heavens, as if sighting the deity they deemed responsible for their brother's death, and fired three volleys that split the stillness. The shots were a wartime custom used to announce that the battlefield was clear of the dead and that the killing could recommence. The rifles prophesied more death, more funerals, and more weeping mothers.

A lone soldier raised a bugle to play Taps and the vibrating melancholic tones strained the emotions of even the most stoic. In the reverent vacuum of the bugler's last note, the honor guard responded like crisp marionettes strung by a master's hand. They recovered each corner of the flag from the casket and then snapped it so taut that it startled a nearby mourner. They folded it twice lengthwise and then began a series of folds that transformed the flag into a shaped triangle.

The officer affectionately placed three shell casings into the folded flag, each representing a volley. The folds were meant to conceal the blood-red stripes and leave nine shining stars exposed on the double-sided blue canvas. Thus folded, the implication was that God's creation of stars and sky is the only thing to be treasured; the blood stripes, symbolizing the sacrifice of man, are minimized. After taking the folded flag from the officer, the Sergeant knelt before the childless mother to present a wrinkleless flag.

Then he whispered words few could hear, but I found myself lip-syncing in memorized silence: "This flag is presented on behalf of a grateful nation and the United States Army as a token of appreciation for your loved one's honorable and faithful service." The mother heard the same familiar tune in his words as she did the day we regretted to inform her.

The funeral director dismissed the crowd, but a few people stopped briefly to lay a rose upon the casket. Only selected family members saw what came next. Two perspiring funeral directors in ill-fitting suits used specialized tools to winch the casket into the grave a few inches at a time. Mrs. Addison stood from her chair and walked to the edge of the hole. With each click of the ratchet, she leaned dangerously close to her son until she was once again on her knees in the dirt. When she finally seemed convinced that Steven would remain there, she held a rose suspended above the casket and dropped it just above his heart.

Afterward, I returned to my car. The temperature was almost 100 degrees, but I closed the windows and sat shaking. We'd had four wars since World War II, but authentic peace still eludes us. In Korea, we pretended to have won. In Vietnam, the lessons of war sank in the Tonkin Gulf. In Iraq, we were told "Mission accomplished." Was it different this time? I didn't know. Maybe it was different this time. Maybe this time, it was worth Addison's sacrifice. There was only one way I'd know. I had to go. I had 25 reasons to go. This was all I knew to do.

CHAPTER 2

LIVING A COMFORTABLE LIFE

On the last Friday morning of 2007 my neighbor woke to retrieve the *Sacramento Bee* newspaper from her doorstep. Ten minutes later she put on her housecoat, wrapped a scarf around her head, and walked outside to write a number on her whiteboard. The new number warned that American war deaths were approaching 4,000, and based on the increased notifications I was doing, I wasn't surprised. President Bush declared that we would find our "New Way Forward" that year, so he ordered 20,000 additional soldiers into Iraq and extended the tour of duty for nearly every existing troop in the country. The press called it the "surge" and, with 899 troops killed in action, it became the deadliest year for the U.S. military since Vietnam.

I awakened that morning as I did each weekday, at 6:15 a.m., inside the master bedroom of our five-bedroom stucco home positioned at the entrance of a predictable California cul-de-sac. I collected my newspaper from my front porch and read it while hunched over a bowl of Special K cereal. After breakfast I put on khaki pants, a starched blue shirt with a Disney character necktie and slipped my feet into tasseled loafers. Then I put a mug of hot tea in the cup holder of my minivan and drove it from my three-car garage to meet my vanpool of five nurses in the local Safeway parking lot. By 8 a.m., I was clocking in at the downtown civilian hospital where I worked my "day-job" as the chaplain for women and children services.

I started Monday, as I always did, in our second floor Neonatal Intensive Care Unit (NICU) caring for the various families of our fifty patients.

"Nick-you," as hospital staff members called it, was a world of wires, IV bottles, and back-lit beds, a close-quarter place where doctors, nurses and respiratory therapists would squeeze themselves through a tangled web of tubes to deliver highly specialized healthcare to the tiniest people you have ever seen.

On occasion, each of the four glass-enclosed units could seem like a movie set where an extra-terrestrial was being examined by scores of scientists and doctors. The NICU and the adjoining Labor and Delivery department were either the happiest places on earth or the saddest places on earth. Happy families filled the waiting room with balloons to celebrate baby's homecoming day. But about once a week, I sat in a private room with sad families while they rocked their premature baby into heaven. Fortunately during that final week of December, most of our preemie patients were what the nurses affectionately called "Feed and grow." These happy babies would go home healthy as long as they were allowed the proper incubation time to eat and grow

While the NICU had been quiet, my responsibilities in the Pediatric cancer ward became especially busy early in the week when Benton Regello was readmitted. Benton was an 8-year-old boy whose chemotherapy treatments had given him the permanently rounded face and balding head of Charlie Brown. He had been blinded by a tumor at 15 months and hospitalized multiple times during the past 26 months for chemo and surgeries, but it seemed as though Benton was beating the odds. However, on that Friday before Christmas, he developed a headache and quickly lost consciousness. His mom rushed him to our hospital where tests revealed a large tumor had hemorrhaged and caused a stroke.

A few days later, I found Benton curled up in his bed with his eyes open but not looking into this world. His parents, Bob and Jeanne, had joined their bed with their only child and lay stretched alongside him, stroking his head and whispering things I could not hear.

Benton had suffered more seizures and was actively dying.

"We've tried to say our good-byes," his mom explained. "But I know he's worried about us. He knew he would go to heaven, but he didn't want to go there alone. Could you say a prayer so he will know he's not alone?"

My prayer came from the Psalms. "Where can I go from your Spirit? Where can I flee from your presence? If I go up to the heavens, you are there."

I knew the prayer well because it was the same prayer I'd prayed at Addison's funeral five months earlier at the graveyard while a giant flag flapped from a towering crane. I was sensing that it would be a prayer I'd say many more times in the next year.

Throughout that day, I also visited bedridden pregnant women in the High Risk Maternity unit and made brief stops in the Emergency Room checking for new pediatric admits. Finally when the clock read 5 p.m., I did the reverse commute to be home for dinner at 6 p.m. After our meal, my wife and I sat in our double recliner while she graded homework papers for her fourth grade class, and I wrote my syndicated newspaper column centering on my life experiences as a chaplain.

Simultaneous to my life as a civilian hospital chaplain, I served as a chaplain in the Air National Guard. On the first weekend of each month, I put on the Airman Battle Uniform (ABU), a service-distinctive camouflage uniform favored by military members for its denim feel, and assumed my position as the Group Chaplain for the 162nd Combat Communications Group, California Air National Guard.

Between my work with Air National Guard, the newspaper column, the hospital work and my wife's teaching job, we enjoyed a routine that paid pretty well. "Life was good and just getting gooder," as the saying goes.

However, the multiple death notifications were haunting me to go to Iraq and see what the war was about. But before I could volunteer, I needed help to explain my logic aloud to my wife. I found that help in a video from the hospital library called "Baghdad ER."

On that last Friday of 2007 I came through the garage door and gave my wife, Becky, our usual barrage of three quick kisses. She returned my affections with her usual three-squeeze hug and then asked what I was hiding behind my back. Becky has an analytical mind that she gets from a half-German father who has spent the past 45 years preaching Southern Baptist theology from the same Sacramento pulpit. She's an independent thinker whose petite 5'3" frame gives you no warning of the feministic bent she found in the sixties. At our wedding in early 1980, she refused to let her father "give" her away. She said she wasn't a commodity to give away like "the house" or "the car." So a word to the wise: don't call her "the wife." And most of all, don't describe her as the "chaplain's lovely wife." I love her like there is no tomorrow and she's not one to be swayed by flattery.

She took the cassette from my hand and gave it a sideways glance that said she saw no subtlety in my approach. The video jacket boasted that the HBO documentary captured "the humanity, hardships and heroism of the U.S. military and medical personnel of the 86th Combat Support Hospital . . ."

She brushed her hair behind her ears like she does when she's ready to rebut my altruisms. I could tell that she wanted to know *Why this video? Why this particular day?* I knew she expected a thoughtful answer, not my usual Public Affairs script. Nevertheless I proffered the latter: "The Air Force is asking for chaplain volunteers at their hospital inside Balad Air Base, Iraq. Specifically, they are requesting a 'hospital-trained chaplain' for a four-month deployment in a Level I trauma center."

She gave me no hint as to what she was thinking. All I knew was that I had ignored her recent hints to retire and she was thankful that I'd avoided harm's way for 20 years. Whatever she was thinking, I knew she had an innate preference for facts and followed them like a topological map through the Alps. However, my logic blazes a more circuitous and freewheeling route. I was thinking that after 20 years of military life outside the war zones, it was my turn to volunteer. So, I bulldozed her with the remaining facts from the military website: "The hospital does over 1,200 surgical procedures a month. They help everyone – military, civilians and contractors, as well as Iraqi soldiers, police, civilians and even detainees."

"What makes you special?" she asked. "I mean, why are you the only one to do this?"

She knew the answer, but I still pointed to my hospital I.D. badge because I was one of the few Air National Guard chaplains with hospital experience. I also completed the essential training program called Clinical Pastoral Education where I worked as a yearlong chaplain resident at the University of California, Davis Medical Center. I'd spent countless on-call hours talking to the victims of all kinds of violence: gangs, police, robbery, and child abuse. The program taught me to affirm the patient's personal beliefs by helping them to reconnect with the spiritual component of their lives.

Perhaps most important, I learned that the chaplain's role is not one of proselytizing. In other words, I could believe that Jesus is my friend – and even theirs – but it would be an ethical violation to force such an unsolicited view on a patient. The training caused me to shed much of my evangelical assumptions, while Becky maintained much of hers.

"Let's watch it after dinner, okay?" she suggested and then she ushered me to the kitchen table that she'd set with colorless paper plates and napkins. We worked our way through half of a grocery store rotisserie chicken and then reclined in our loveseat to watch the video. The documentary showed real doctors working on seriously wounded soldiers and a chaplain struggling to say the right words to the soldier. I stole a look at Becky, but couldn't make out what she was thinking. She was either frozen over with the logic I was presenting or she was majorly pissed that I was making her decide about this. With credits rolling, she blurted a question that had me betting on the latter option.

"Why do you want to volunteer?"

I faced her in the chair to see that hers wasn't a question of demand, but a pleading for help to process the idea. However, I wasn't in the mood for processing because I was so ready to get on the first plane that I would have parachuted into Iraq if necessary.

She recognized my manic anxiety and suggested we snap our proud pup, Chewy, to a leash and walk through the parkside trail that crisscrosses our subdivision. The path took us to the subdivision park where we stopped on the edge of the kidney-shaped pond. Becky pointed to the cattle egrets and their offspring as she quickly emphasized the multisided meaning of volunteer.

"What makes you think you'll be the only volunteer here?" she blurted. "What about me? Aren't you asking me to volunteer for 120 days of solo parenting?"

I didn't have much of an answer, so I diverted the conversation through everything from car problems to household repairs. Becky responded to my litany by taking a seat on a nearby park bench and patting the place beside her. I sat where instructed, but wasn't smart enough to let her speak first.

"It doesn't seem fair that we should enjoy a newly remodeled kitchen with updated appliances and hardwood flooring while so many troops are being fit for prosthetic appliances or measured for hardwood caskets."

"I know," she said.

She knew, but I still added more to my growing pile of survivor's guilt.

"How come we get to drive a new car while so many soldiers ride in target-rich, lightly armored Humvees? I sleep with you while the soldiers sleep with rifles."

"I know! I know!" she said. She didn't want to hear any more about the disparity between my stateside life and the deployed life.

"Then, what are you afraid of?"

"Two things. First, I'm afraid you'll die."

"Don't worry. There hasn't been a chaplain killed in the line of duty since Vietnam, so don't count on getting my Serviceman's Group Life Insurance."

She showed no appreciation for my deflection of choice – gallows humor. These weren't things she found funny. She'd been afraid of the death possibility ever since I joined the Air Force, but this was the first time she'd been so blunt. She knew better than most how routinely death calls on a soldier's home. She knew the possibilities of receiving midnight visitors telling her that I, or our Marine son, had been killed in action.

"Norris." She stood, her stiff blue-eyed gaze churning to shred my trumped-up confidence. She was petite in size, but she wasn't going to be bullied or trivialized. "I really need to know why you must do this now." she said. "The children and I need you here. Nicole is flopping through high school. Michael is struggling in basic training. Brittney is a pregnant single parent on the verge of homelessness and Sara is planning her wedding." She'd covered the bases from youngest to oldest.

Two could play the guilt game, so I stood too.

"Are you really asking the obvious?" I asked. "I want to know how these men are dying. I need to know if this war is worth the cost."

I turned away from her and set a cadence homeward that said I'd delivered the final word. Becky followed but remained uncharacteristically quiet. She's not fond of the slightest profanity from me, so she walked a little ways behind me. Chewy pulled me forward to greet each passing dog, and when we were nearly home, Becky finally blurted, "You can't go. You promised me that you'd stay around to raise your new puppy. Maybe we should give Chewy to that nurse friend of yours who likes him so much."

It was my turn to be quiet. She has no affinity for animals, but I knew she didn't hate them. She didn't mean this. She was playing her last card.

Back in the house, I resumed my place at the table staring at a newspaper I'd already read twice while Becky cleared dinner from our newly tiled countertops and scrubbed the grout like someone looking for better luck from a lotto scratcher. I stared through our nook window, my eyes following the vacuum sweeping our kidney-shaped pool while I searched for better ways to float my deployment logic.

Why did any soldier want to go to war? Perhaps their recruiter whispered the promise of money or the sex appeal of the uniform. Perhaps a wartime video game told them that a reset button would bring an extra life. I didn't comprehend their volunteerism, but I needed to know. Perhaps they trusted that their battle armor would be worthy of its name or that they would get a parade if they fell on a grenade. Maybe their fantasies promised them that young women would cry over their caskets and old vets in crumpled war hats would salute their rainy day hearse. All I could think about was that some of those soldiers would return in the pressurized hold of a cargo plane and I'd be left standing with a uniformed team on their poorly lit home porch listening for the guttural screams of their family.

When Becky couldn't find another space in the kitchen to scrub, she joined me at the table. This time, she took both my hands as she detailed reason number two about why I should stay home.

"I'm not so much afraid that you will die. I'm more afraid that you'll come back, different."

"Different?"

"You know, like before," she said. She was struggling with a voice that was breaking into a hoarse whisper, "Like what happened to you before – in Stockton." She'd dared cross the boundary of "before."

A sliver of Cleveland Elementary in Stockton California returned with a jolt. Becky was right and she had every reason to expect that Iraq would also bring on changes too. Volunteering had its pitfalls. The woulda, coulda, shouldas that followed the schoolyard shooting became parasites infecting my daily thoughts. I had become, in my wife's words, "different than before." My wife knew that the madman who shot kids like he was shooting carnival ducks on a pinwheel had changed her husband forever. Volunteers get hurt, too. Bullets aren't just hardened projectiles that shatter bodies. They ricochet into the shadowed places of the soul to remind you that every aspect of life is theirs for the taking. Not a day passed in the year following the shooting in which I didn't think about the kids and not a night darkened without them surveilling my dreams. Even now, a simple school bell or emergency siren brings me back to Stockton.

But I stubbornly held a different opinion. "I'll be fine," I said, and I broke loose of her hands to fill a glass at the refrigerator's ice dispenser.

"That was 20 years ago," I said, now shouting over the crushing ice. "Besides," I claimed, "those kids were innocent. They didn't volunteer to die. Soldiers make their own decisions about life."

I suppose I was pleading for dismissal of her argument on the absurd grounds that the deaths of people who comprehend their risks are less tragic. When I returned to the table, I finally raised both hands and admitted that I wasn't quite sure why I wanted to go.

That was a lie. I did know. I wanted to go to Iraq to fathom the sorrow that had become my job to know, not just regret. More than that, I wanted to tell families that I had seen how their loved ones handled the act of dying. I wanted to be able to answer the questions families asked: Was my son brave? Did my daughter have misgivings about the war? Did they feel honor? Or did they just feel cold?

Now the questions were being put on me. There in my kitchen, I sat stuttering at my wife's question. Why?

"I want to go because…" I pulled in some air to inflate my courage. "I want to go because the Air Force is asking for a hospital chaplain, and I can't sit here when I know I can help."

I stopped at that, unable to state it more profoundly, but it must have been enough because after another week of detailed discussion, Becky came to me while I was at my home desk answering email. She placed her hands on my shoulder and flatly said, "You need to go. You need to feel you've done your share. I understand."

At that point, I composed an email response to the Chief of Chaplain's office volunteering to serve as the senior chaplain at the Air Force Field Hospital in Balad, Iraq. I proofread my words to be sure I was clearly stating the parameters of my volunteerism and then asked Becky if she would press the 'send' button. Her index finger hovered over the keyboard in some hesitation until she finally gave the 'send' button a definitive push. With all she had and with all she knew, she understood.

CHAPTER 3

BOOTS ON THE GROUND

On December 30, 2008, after nearly a year of preparation and 48 hours of flights, I finally arrived in Balad, Iraq. I'd been on the ground four jet-lagged hours and was going through the newcomer briefing when the outgoing hospital chapel team sent word inviting me to rendezvous with them just outside the swinging emergency room doors of the Air Force Field Hospital.

I got some quick directions and made my way to the hospital of the 332d Expeditionary Medical Group where I was greeted by Staff Sergeant Terry Mueth, a lanky and unassuming white kid from Ohio. Beside Mueth, stood the unarmed and gently rounded African-American Chaplain, Major Wendell Roamer. Roamer was a week from being called my predecessor and only a few months away from being named 2008 Air National Guard Chaplain of the Year.

Roamer gave me a hearty backslap and dubbed me his "new best friend." I smiled at the well-known deployment slang for replacement, a term originating from the commander's policy that no one went home until their replacement arrived on station. Roamer was going home now.

"Glad you're here," Roamer said. He had the buttery voice of a DJ, but the words I heard in my jetlagged ears sounded more like "Yada, yada, yada."

"Wish we could have met under better circumstances," I muttered. I added a few more of those things you say when your automatic pilot is on the forced-smile setting.

Roamer nodded and then shifted his voice into a professional whisper. "I'm going to take you in here." He pointed his shaved head in the direction of a swinging set of windowed doors. "I think you need to see our process when someone dies."

I was awake now. I thought I'd come for a simple building tour, but nobody asked for my vote, so we followed all 6 feet 6 inches of Roamer through the prefab doors that split the word "Emergency." Roamer walked me a few steps past the nursing station to "Trauma Room #1." The room was nothing more than a curtained closet big enough to contain a gurney and a handful of bedside staff members.

This was where I first saw 20-year-old Army Specialist Joseph Lot. His face reflected the pink shade of someone who had seen little of Iraq's relentless sun. His haircut, shaved "hoo'yah" tight, bragged the hard-nose look of "battle ready." Aside from a pinprick bullet hole through his skull, he seemed unmarked. There was no blood. Lot looked as though he was enjoying the afternoon nap that I desperately needed.

"He's categorized as 'expectant.' We are only doing comfort care now," Roamer whispered. "Expectant" meant that no one in their right medical mind expected Lot to survive. "Comfort care" meant the same thing it meant in the pediatric hospital when I had prayed over little Benton. There were no fixes, and doctors would work only to relieve symptoms, optimize comfort and bring final relief. It meant that we would wait on Lot's timetable no matter how long it took and no matter how tired we became.

"He's hanging on," Roamer said. "The staff figured he'd be gone hours ago."

I glanced around to see dozens of men and women in colorful scrubs standing ready, maybe even anxious, to escort Lot to our morgue. Yet they stood lingering to honor the moment of death. They appeared to postpone their own breathing, waiting for the chaplain to say Lot's final prayer and waiting for the moment when the honor guard would lower the American flag on Lot's blanketed body.

We stood for a few minutes without talking, and then Roamer gathered us behind the nursing station countertop. He raised his voice a tick over a whisper and explained that Lot had been a part of a four-man squad from the 3rd Brigade Combat Team, 25th Infantry Division, on a "routine patrol" in the city of Tikrit, Iraq. His squad had stopped to talk to the director of Khadasia General Hospital about upgrading the city's water plant. The squad leader ordered Lot to remain with their Humvee while the others went inside to talk to the director. Lot assumed a defensive stance with his upper torso protruding from the gunner's hatch, and when his squad returned 20 minutes later, he was slumped over his 50-caliber machine gun with a sniper bullet in his skull. His battle buddies loaded him on a Blackhawk helicopter and sent him ninety miles south to our emergency room. Since then, Lot had lingered and the ER staff had done little in eight hours but wait for his departure and my arrival.

Just as Roamer finished explaining all this, we watched a hospital orderly place a folded body bag under Lot's gurney. The bag told us all that the final waiting had begun. The silence was so inescapable that it seemed as if I could hear men scratching their twelve-hour shadow beards. A medical technician, slouched behind a computer at the nurses' station, popped his knuckles and another 30 minutes passed.

Unfortunately, Lot wasn't ready to find comfort. He wouldn't die. Not yet. He had no timetable. So we all waited. The doctors, the medics and the grieving soldiers were assembled from various military branches, but we waited as one body. Something told me that if I were to become a good combat chaplain, I would have to master this art of waiting. I took that moment to ask myself what kind of chaplain I was planning to be for the dying. What role would I play? Would I say, "You're a hero, son"? Would I play it safe and disperse Bible quotes like lawn fertilizer? Would I coax an "expectant" soldier through a darkened tunnel or commend her to an eternal light? Would I convey certainty that there was a light? Or would I stumble in the shadows? Would people say I was only there to play the chaplain role described in Burdon's Sky Pilot song?

He blesses the boys as they stand in line
The smell of gun grease and their bayonets they shine
He's there to help them all that he can
To make them feel wanted he's a good holy man
Sky pilot.....sky pilot
How high can you fly?
You'll never, never, ever reach the sky

Something about my role told me I was supposed to be sure of these things.

Suddenly the radio squawked about an incoming American patient with a head wound and vital signs that sounded much like Lot's. Unable to keep their day frozen in time, the staff moved Lot into an adjoining room. Dying soldiers create discomfort among those who train so well to avoid such ends. I've watched enough children die to know that death can't linger in a trauma room too long before it surrenders the stench of defeat. Lot's disappearance hinted that the pace wouldn't slow and that the horror show would go on.

Roamer gave a move toward the door that hinted we should make room for scrambling staff. Mueth grabbed Roamer's arm and turned toward me.

"Are you okay, Chaplain Burkes?" Mueth asked.

"Yes, thanks," I muttered in the voice of someone who perceived himself a good liar.

They shook their heads.

"You're a bit pale," said Roamer. My exhaustion had caught up with me and now my whitening face bore a strong resemblance to Lot's flat-line expression.

"Sit down," Mueth ordered. His command was slightly out of place from a non-commissioned officer, so I hesitated.

"Take a seat, Chaplain," Roamer said and slid a chair under me while the hospital veterans reached a committee consensus that Mueth would escort me to my new billeting.

Roamer brought me bottled water and then he walked us outside to the staff truck where he tucked me into the passenger side and gave the fender two giddy-up slaps. Mueth slid behind the wheel and gunned the engine. A few minutes later we drove into a gated housing area that resembled a mobile-home park. Two gravel-covered acres surrounded dozens of buildings called "pods." I counted at least fifty, with each pod approximating a four-door cargo container elevated two feet off the ground with concrete blocks.

"H6 is great housing because it doesn't take much mortar fire," Mueth said. His excitement mimicked a hotel clerk booking a room far from a noisy ice machine. Was there a safe place here, I wondered? It felt like he was avoiding the irony that Lot had been killed while visiting a hospital or that our pods bore a souped-up resemblance to the hospital's portable morgue.

Mueth briefed the amenities of each hooch. "You got two sets of bunk beds, an air conditioner, a window and an outside door. No maid service on weekends." He snickered planning his next line. "Or, for that matter, any other day of the week." I gave a polite chuckle as he stopped the boss' F150 only a few hundred yards from a fence separating us from the passenger terminal I'd transited six hours earlier. Mueth grabbed my bags from the truck and heaved them up three porch steps into my pod, placing them next to a pile of what looked like unclaimed luggage.

"Have a good night, sir," he said. I returned his salute and closed the door to the prefab smell of linoleum. When my eyes adjusted to the 60-watt light bulb, I saw what resembled a college dorm room. Each side mirrored the other. There were two bunk sets, locking metal wardrobes, and nightstands supporting gooseneck lamps. I peeled my uniform from my sweaty torso and piled it shin-high on the sandy floor and climbed onto a plastic-wrapped mattress. I lay there for an hour encased in fearful daydreams. I was past exhaustion and felt like a NASCAR driver slammed up against the inside wall.

My mental engines were racing to grip the track stretched out before me until I finally blurted into the darkness, "Where the hell am I? What the hell have I done?"

No one answered my first question, so I answered it myself. "I'm in Balad, Iraq, located in the Sunni Triangle forty miles north of Baghdad." My voice sounded logical, and I was starting to believe myself when I heard a dull thump outside. I looked at my watch and realized that I didn't have time to ponder my second question. Besides, it had no answer yet.

On New Year's Day 2009, I awoke assuming three things to be true. First, a Pennsylvania National Guard chaplain like myself got the order to regretfully inform Lot's parents. Second, my house-coated neighbor lady had retrieved the *Sacramento Bee* from her flowerbed and turned to write "4081" on her whiteboard. My third assumption was that I was alone in the room. I wasn't.

⅄ ⅄ ⅄

The vibrating hum of the heater protruding above my bunk had masked the late-night entry of the man who was standing a few feet from where I was sleeping.

When the man noticed me startle, he prompted calmness with a downturned hand. "It's okay. I'm just your old roommate." He chuckled at himself. "I'm leaving tonight, but you'll get a new roommate soon." The man was Air Force Major Mark Tidwell. He had spent the past six months working as the commander's executive officer, and he'd returned to our hooch late in the night to collect his gear for his plane ride home.

Tidwell had the political face endemic in a commander's office. His lantern-shaped jaw was forged with certainty, but his affable humor invited disclosure. After hearing most of his muffled introduction, I dug my sleep plugs from my ears and asked, "Any advice for a newcomer?"

"First off," he said, "I wouldn't sleep with earplugs if I were you. I'll bet you didn't hear the attack alarm last night."

I answered with a fully awakened expression that hinted at my need for details.

"We had a mortar hit near our shower facility last night. It didn't explode, but you may have heard the thud."

"Is that what that noise was?" I muttered.

"Don't worry," he said. "EOD is digging it out right now."

The news that the Explosive Ordinance Disposal team was working outside our hooch brought me up on my elbows. Outwardly, I presented my roomie with a so-what shrug, but inside I echoed my bedtime question: What the hell have I done?

"Second piece of advice," Tidwell said in rising tones. "Involve yourself in something besides work, and your days will feel shorter." Tidwell was parroting the tone of the Balad welcome brief – "Don't count the days, make the days count." The mortar had suddenly increased my mathematical skills. This was Day 2, and I had 119 remaining days.

I swung my feet from under my scratchy army blanket and onto the dusty linoleum floor to watch my "old roommate" pack away the comfort improvements he'd engineered. He was folding the blue bedspread he'd used to partition his bottom bunk into a private tent by pinching one side of the bedspread into the overhead bunk and draping it into a privacy curtain. He'd suspended a battery-powered reading light from the inside slats to create the cocooned feel of an Amtrak sleeper berth. I imagined him the type who, before lights-out, kissed his index finger and tagged the family pictures he'd inserted into the slats of his overhanging bunk. The last item he packed was the bedside throw rug he used to do his barefoot morning stretches.

"Straight up, though," he added, "There's really not much to do here. I read books, go to the gym and watch a lot of DVDs." And with a few last pleasantries, Tidwell packed up his computer, zipped his bursting bags, and headed toward the doorway to find his plane. "You'll be getting a new roommate in a few days," he said. Then, as quickly as we'd met, Tidwell's forgettable face went out the door.

I stumbled from my bed, stiff from sleeping nearly fourteen hours. It would be the most uninterrupted sleep I'd have during my deployment. I slapped on my flip-flops and gym shorts to make my first trip to the portable showers. Nicknamed the "Cadillac," the showers were perched atop a flat-top trailer bed and were far superior than the tent showers normally used in field conditions. Internet blogs gave the showers a much less favorable name. Built by the vice president's former company, Haliburton, with a no-bid deal called a "sweetheart contract," the poorly wired baths had electrocuted 100 unsuspecting servicemembers and were thus designated "the Dick Cheney Electrocution Showers."

The shocking stories, along with rumors of the shower rapes of both men and women, encouraged me to quickly bathe and return to my hooch to don my newly issued Airman Battle Uniform. The ABU's camouflage pattern made us less visible in low-light environments, a feature which encouraged me to jokingly deny my absence from future staff meetings by claiming that I'd been present in the stealth mode.

Properly attired, I left my hooch and followed the paved walks through expansive gravel lots to the Gilbert Chapel where I'd scheduled my second meeting with Chaplain Roamer. The mortar-resistant chapel served as the mothership for the three base chapels and was located between Green Beans Coffee and the Base Exchange. The chapel was surrounded with a five-room office annex for Chaplain Richard Hearts and seven chaplains, all who were supported by a staff of ten NCOs. Roamer planned our meeting so I could meet Hearts, and since I would have weekly check-ins with him, I was glad to find Gilbert spaced only a quarter mile between my hooch and my hospital office.

We all met in Hearts's office where I shook hands with a wiry, chisel-faced, white man in his mid-fifties. He was much taller than I expected. He projected the controlled appearance of a television newscaster and spoke with a matching voice.

"I trust you had a good trip," he said.

I suppose I did, but I was more anxious to talk to Roamer at the moment than I was to chitchat with the new boss.

"How's our patient?" I asked Roamer.

"Which one?" he said flatly.

When I gave a confused expression, he reminded me of the radio call we'd heard in the ER before Mueth escorted me home. The incoming patient of the evening had been Private First Class Benjamin Talbot. The 20-year-old was in Iraq only two months when his unit was attacked and Talbot took a slug in the head.

"Where was he from?" I asked.

"Stockon, California," Roamer replied.

I looked at the boss' unreadable expression. Balad chaplains had become used to death, but my hands had tightened into a ball. Stockton was within driving range from my home. If I'd been home, I may have been the chaplain assigned to tell the newlywed Mrs. Talbot that she would be raising their eight-month-old son alone.

"We lost both him and Lot during the night," Roamer said. "But things have slowed quite a bit over the past few weeks. It won't be like this every day."

"Do you have everything you need?" Hearts said with a commanding change of subject.

"Yes, sir. Squared away," I said. I had everything I needed, but I also had a sense I had nothing I needed.

By week's end, the outgoing chapel staff had boarded their flight home and my metamorphosis was complete. I was no longer a pediatric chaplain wearing a Bugs Bunny necktie entertaining giggling kids in a hospital play-room with dancing animal marionettes. I was a combat chaplain who slept within range of enemy mortars and served alongside doctors wearing holstered side arms just below their dangling stethoscopes.

CHAPTER 4

THE SLOW DAYS OF WAR

If you had followed me through my first two weeks as the senior chaplain at the Air Force Field Hospital, you'd have thought my job was butt-numbingly slow. The weather was cool and the sun pleasantly warm enough that it became easy to cruise along on the surface of normal by slurping big gulps of iced chai and shopping all three of the base exchanges (BX). Between my shopping breaks, I visited various patients with infections, flu, appendicitis or broken appendages they'd received playing "cutthroat volleyball," but I saw nothing of the serious sort I'd seen the first week. It had been inordinately quiet ever since Roamer and Mueth boarded their flight home.

But in a hospital where the main business is mortally-wounded soldiers or tragically injured Iraqis, you pray for things to remain slow. How would you pray for anything else? You don't want people hurt just to give you someone to comfort. You don't want people dying just so you can say a prayer and wear your most pastoral look.

To that end, I avoided using the word "slow" because the medical staff was amusingly superstitious about the word. They lightheartedly banned the "S" word, saying it could jinx a perfectly good day. They knew, of course, that slow days could not predict what the very next minute could bring. They knew that each day had the potential to be hours of boredom interrupted by minutes of sheer terror.

The most exciting day of my second week came when I watched my new chaplain assistant, Staff Sergeant David Peoples, amble down the loading ramp of the C130 transport plane wearing a 50-pound pack and the same dazed expression I'd worn a few weeks prior. The man was a horse looking for a rider. He swung his flak vest and helmet along his side like dirty laundry.

Like me, he'd probably kissed a sleepy wife goodbye, caught a taxi to an airport swarming with holiday travelers and boarded a flight to Baltimore. I even thought it possible that he gave his lunch order to the same surly waitress who served me at BWI before I walked a half-mile to the military terminal and transferred to a government chartered 747.

Then, he spent the next ten hours on a plane of 350 soldiers hopscotching across Europe until its final stop at Al Udeid Air Base in Qatar for crew rest. From Qatar, he sifted his way through thousands of soldiers in the combat assembly line divided into "chalks" of 55 people and boarded a web-seated C130 camouflage transport plane bound for various destinations in our Area of Responsibility or AOR. Five hours after Peoples boarded that plane, I watched it make the customary "combat landing" in a series of aerobatic dips and zags, done at 150-knot, on a 5-degree glide slope into the busiest airfield in the world.

Peoples was a sanitary engineer from Youngstown, Ohio, who greeted me wearing a non-issue scarf and goggles around his neck. I guessed that his garb meant either he wasn't expecting the dampened feel of an urban base or that he'd worked a full day and left his municipal garbage truck in long-term airport parking. His initial appearance suggested little of the sensitivity required in hospital ministry. He was a slow-moving, 45-year-old, balding white target whose 6 feet, 4 inches surpassed me by a few inches and dwarfed my 190-pound frame. He wore a farmer's tan and walked with the characteristic slump of man carrying a full load all day.

While his chalk assembled for the customary briefing, I took a chair to review an email he'd sent and weighed my early impressions of him. Something made me sure that I was going to like him. Since the role of the Air Force chaplain assistant is primarily a clerical one, I supposed that he'd do okay. Peoples was not there to be a "junior chaplain" or counselor. His job was to help with administrative tasks such as filing reports, requisitioning materials and arranging the chapel altar for worship and communion. He would do worship bulletins, compose PowerPoint presentations, and inventory chapel equipment–all routine tasks, slow and mundane.

Oh yes, one more thing. Peoples was there to carry a gun because my Geneva Convention status as noncombatant prohibited me from doing so. It was his job to protect me with his life. I wasn't sure of his marksmanship ability, but I supposed his large frame would offer good cover. All of this might explain his first remark after the briefing.

"I gotta get me a weapon," he said.

"You won't need one," I said. "The boss says sidearms are issued only if we are going off base, and we won't be doing that."

"That ain't right," he mumbled.

"Maybe not," I said but offered him a consoling trip to the dining hall. Somewhere from under his thin layer of dust, he flashed a faint smile to my suggestion.

We drove the boss' truck to the dining hall and walked into a guarded facility about the size of a Home Depot. It was one of five base dining halls that served four daily meals and made the average Hometown Buffet look like a soup kitchen. Peoples piled a plate with enough potato and tuna salad to put me in a mayonnaise coma. He plopped a double cheeseburger and fries on his second plate. Twenty minutes later, we both walked out of the dining hall sipping milkshakes, and I decided he might just be my culinary mentor.

"Let's take the base windshield tour," I said. I'd been there only a few weeks and already become the old guy who shows the new guy the ropes.

Peoples stopped in place and fixed me with an unfiltered look that followed me to the driver's door.

"Oh, come on! It'll help you get through your jet lag," I said. It was the same refried advice given all newcomers.

Peoples took the passenger seat and settled in for the sixty-minute blur of base amenities, including a movie theater with a Subway, sandwiched by a Burger King and Pizza Hut. He read every sign aloud, including the reader board posted outside the gym/entertainment complex that promised dance lessons with USO morale concerts. When we passed the two Olympic-sized swimming pools, indoor and outdoor, he noted something about the temptation that a bikini-clad soldier might bring to deployed men. He saw my head nod but missed my rolling eyes.

Peoples was soon sinking his knuckles deep into his eye sockets. He seemed astonished at how easily our government could reproduce the sense of normalcy on a base with more than 25,000 people, a place sprouting fat factories like Cinnabon and Taco Bell. Bases like Balad have so many amenities that the rank-and-file warriors describe those stationed in them as REMFs (Rear Echelon Mother Fuddies.) REMFs are those guys who live in relative comfort either because they've worked the system or because their job requires it. Most Air Force chaplains work in the REMF category, along with medical and legal personnel.

Peoples gained a hypnotized expression from whizzing past the five-story high guard towers lining our perimeter road like connect-the-dots, so I promised I'd take him back to his hooch after we made just one more stop.

"Sorry," I said, as I adjusted my major's cap under the afternoon glare. "I suppose this is like drinking from a fire hose, but we still need to see the hospital."

"Yes, sir," he said, but he'd deflated most of the "sir."

We drove another half-mile and stopped at the hospital guard shack to show our IDs and then parked inside the fenced compound that surrounded the hospital. We stepped from the truck into a gravel-covered parking area the size of a Super Wal-Mart parking lot. Near the entrance, I pointed toward a big metal box called a "refer," a refrigerated portable morgue.

"That's where we put the bodies until we can send them home."

Peoples hadn't talked much that morning, nor would he on most mornings, but he did manage to shoot me the first of his famously slanted what-the-hell looks.

"We escort the bodies into that refer before they are sent home," I said.

The refer was the first stop in the process of sending the bodies back into my stateside turf of funeral homes and veteran's cemeteries. Not far from the refer, I pointed out a bomb shelter which was supposed to protect those caught in the open during an attack.

"They bomb the dead?" he asked. That comment evoked my what-the-hell look, but he chose not to see it.

A series of walled walkways led to the hospital door. Like all the Balad buildings, the hospital was surrounded with 12-foot concrete blast walls that seemed more fitting for a squash super tournament, or even a maze for gifted children. The barriers were staggered just far enough from the buildings to allow for pedestrians and were spray-painted with artwork vetted by the hospital commander.

Inside the front door, a Nigerian civilian contractor flashed a toothy smile and greeted us with "Hello, Chap-lin." He took Peoples' ID and gave him a clip-on visitor badge in exchange. Peoples wanted to get chatty, but I nudged him forward into the rectangle of hospital hallways where he took off toward the men's room like his lunch coffee caught up with him. He returned to the hallway still trying to button his fly.

"Hey, I got a question," he said. The introductory statement would become his verbal moniker. He hooked a thumb in the direction of a passing doctor wearing Bart Simpson scrubs and asked, "How come they get to wear those?"

"The rules are different here," I said.

He gave me a well practiced "Duh, Sherlock" stare. Undeterred, I offered an example.

"For instance, this entire compound is a no-hat-no-salute area. And obviously there's a different dress code that is supposed to make the patients feel more at home."

"Uh-huh," he said. "Right."

"One more thing," I added as we passed the dining hall. "During our twelve-hour shifts we're confined to the hospital, so we have to eat in the hospital dining room."

He peeked inside the 20-seat dining cubby and yawned in the midst of squeezing out another, "Uh-huh. Right."

Hoping to curb his fatigue, I yanked him through a round robin of quick office introductions that included the hospital commander, his deputy, the chief nurse and the hospital security manger. I could tell he was losing their names just past each handshake, so I ducked him into our office where he slumped into the recliner like a returning king. He swept an inspecting look over the 150-square-foot room that he'd be responsible to maintain. He grabbed the TV remote, threw CNN on our 42-inch widescreen TV, and extended an upturned hand to sample the frigid air current flowing from our window air conditioner.

"All the comforts, right?" I asked. "There is a small gym downstairs. If the gym doesn't offer enough torture," I cracked, "you'll find one of Saddam's old torture chambers down there too." My comments brought no chuckles from the big man, but they did manage to bring him to his feet and back on tour.

Outside my office, Peoples noticed the international housekeeping staff of Third Country Nationals, commonly called "TCNs." The young Indian men were busy wiping the dusty walls and scrubbing muddied boot tracks from the tiled floor. TCNs came to Iraq through an arrangement that seemed something just short of peonage. Wages from the first year of their three-year contract paid for their transportation and housing costs. They worked for small international subcontractors that made corporate kingdoms like Haliburton obscenely rich. Whatever dollars the TCN's made never compensated the handful of them who had their feet blown off from random mortar attacks.

Further down the wall from the men, Peoples paused to read the morale cards sent by Mrs. Marino's third-grade class from Strawberry Elementary School in Mill Valley, California. He traced his hand over one of the cards addressed "To Any Soldier," and I thumped one of three nearby 55-gallon drums overflowing with similar cards.

"You'll need to sort through these envelopes for the free phone cards people send." He squinted at my definition of a chaplain assistant's task, so I punctuated the task with a sarcastic *tsk* of my tongue. "Sentiment can be an administrative burden in a warzone."

We kept walking down the hall, making right turns until we pushed through swinging doors and into the nearly empty emergency room. We stopped to make small talk with a few unit clerks who were sharing pictures from their supposedly alcohol-free New Year's Eve party. A doctor pushed aside his charting duties to hail us.

"Hey, Chap!" called Dr. Joseph Deavers.

"Hey, Czar!"

Deavers, a white doctor in his mid-thirties, called himself "The Trauma Czar," because he was in charge of everything that happened in the Emergency Room, including the daily push-ups he encouraged his staff to do. At 5 feet, 8 inches he maintained his I'm-in-charge stance even on holidays when he wore something far out of regulation–like the cupid outfit he donned for Valentine's Day.

"My new chaplain assistant finally arrived," I said. Peoples extended a hand to shake.

"Got a minute to give him the tour?" I asked.

Deavers nodded and walked us past the red line that separated the nursing station from the trauma area.

"First off," he said, "Our patients come to us aboard Blackhawk medical evacuation helicopters from what most people call MASH units. We call them Combat Support Hospitals, pronounced "cash." The CSH will stabilize the serious injuries and send them to us for surgery. Once we stabilize them, we load them on our medevac plane and send them to our hospital in Germany."

Peoples nodded, but I figured he was already just as lost as I had been when Deavers first explained it to me.

Deavers took a few more steps into the open bay of the ER and pointed into a sparsely equipped room, a span of tiled flooring dowsed with shadows from overhanging florescent lighting. The room seemed a carbon copy in breadth and length to a dozen church coffee halls I'd seen in my ten years of pastoring Baptist congregations.

Deavers pointed to a line on the floor. "When you guys respond to a trauma, you stay behind this red line until *I* call you," he said with a pause on the nominative pronoun. He was the Czar.

"When I call, it will be for you to come to one of these gurneys," he said. "And Chap knows that if I call for you, it'll be bad." Peoples took a hard breath as we both stepped over the red line.

Deavers waved his hand toward the walls where one might expect to see windows, past eight sheeted gurneys inside eight curtained stalls. Two rows of four stalls each faced from opposing sides, giving a passing reminder of thrift store dressing rooms. However, they weren't dressing rooms; they were sequentially numbered trauma bays.

"The space is tight," Deavers said, "but each bay is matched to a team of technicians, nurses and doctors. That matching is what qualifies our dusty building to be called a Level 1 trauma hospital."

Deavers saw my assistant fading, so he tapped him on the chest to stop him mid-yawn. "In the event of a mass causality," he said. "You'll need to page chaplain reinforcements from the main base chapel."

We both sighed with a hint that we'd heard enough for one day, but Deavers wanted to be certain we understood the process. He spent the next 20 minutes showing us the adjoining rooms of MRI machines, X-ray equipment, CAT scans, and a fully equipped blood lab. We gave Deavers the appropriate nods and "wows!" We knew the arrangement far surpassed anything Iraqis had ever seen, but as impressive as it was, Iraqis never needed such a facility before we arrived to liberate them.

When Deavers finally drew a breath, I looked at my watch and announced we had a chapel staff meeting in ten minutes. There was no such meeting, of course. We just needed some time to regroup in our office where Peoples could resume his reclined position.

I drew our door closed, popped open another Diet Pepsi, and offered my lounging assistant the Girl Scout thin mints I'd pulled from the "To-Any-Soldier" boxes stacked outside our office. Amazingly, Peoples' first week was as quiet as mine had been. Our days blended into one another and we started believing that our deployment would be average, boring, and mind-numbingly slow. I only wish that had been so.

CHAPTER 5

DRAMA AND TRAUMA

January 10 felt like a Saturday should and fortunately the feeling lingered most of the morning. Peoples and I ate a big breakfast, called our wives, and finished final preparation for the next day's worship service. Afterward, we sequestered ourselves in our office to watch the NFL playoff games, ready for Saturday to become Sunday. The San Francisco 49ers were knocked out of the playoffs, so I didn't much care who was winning the NFC West. My assistant sorted through the voluminous cards we'd emptied from the hallway barrels while I sat at my desk completing a monthly statistical report. My first three weeks had been as uneventful as Chaplain Roamer had predicted, and my report reflected that.

The report du jour was a fill-in-the-blank statistical form required by my denomination, the Southern Baptist Convention (SBC). While the sports commentators debated the significance of football stats, I sat chewing a pencil eraser wondering whether my denominational stats had much significance. The SBC had moved quite a bit to the right over the years, and I found it problematic to complete the kinds of nickels-and-noses report they required. They asked how many Bible studies I conducted, how many people I baptized, and how many hours I spent counseling. Chaplains often struggle over counseling statistics, because who is to say what constitutes "counseling?" Is it counseling when you tell someone to "Have a nice day?" Probably not, but it might be if a chaplain says it. Do football playoff discussions count as counseling? Probably not, but they might be if a chaplain is conversing with a young soldier during his long day at guard duty. The questions inspire the ambiguous kind of estimates that military members call "pencil-whipping."

I paused at the last question, vaguely aware that there was something I needed to do. What was it? I kept tapping my chin with my pencil eraser as if trying to extract the answer. Then I suddenly remembered that I'd promised to make a call on behalf of Captain Charlotte Anderson, an emergency room nurse.

Anderson was a petite brunette I'd met earlier that morning. She worked in tailored-tight scrubs, and like many ER nurses I knew, kept her energy compressed in a cramped space, ready to expand. With her hair cut in a half circle, it came down on a chin that knew where it wanted to go. On our first meeting, I noticed that her energy had failed her, and she was slumped over the nurses' station desk piercing her computer with a death stare. I knew she was part of the staff that was due to return home that month, so I tossed her a throw-away question to gauge her excitement about going home. She responded by asking me if I did counseling.

A few hours later, she used her lunch break to meander through the hospital corridor and find the door marked "Chaplain." From my desk I watched her stop outside in the hallway and look in both directions as if crossing a dangerous highway. Then she slipped inside, shut the door behind her, perched on my recliner, and proceeded to ask, "Can I get in trouble if…"

I love how that question begins.

No, I don't.

The opening words are designed to probe boundaries, much like enemy insurgents use mortars to probe for weaknesses in a defensive perimeter. It's the kind of legal issue posed by a person who wants to know how far he or she can go. It's the query posed by the teenager sporting a gold WWJD bracelet (What Would Jesus Do?) who wants to know how far he can go with his girlfriend and still keep his virginity. He doesn't honestly want to know what Jesus would do; he wants to know if Jesus is really looking. For the record, He is.

"I took some pictures," she said. She stopped and pulled at the edge of her pants pocket flaps to flatten the wrinkles. "I sent them to my boyfriend in the states."

"What kind of…"

"Nude ones," she said.

"Oh. Well, as long as he keeps them to himself, I don't see..."

"His wife found them," she said.

I resisted doing my Scooby Doo impression and saying, "Ruh-Ro," and settled for a simple, "Oh."

Anderson sat knowing two things. Adultery is a court-martial offense, but anything confessed to a chaplain is completely confidential and inadmissible in court. I knew only one thing. She needed a lawyer, not a chaplain. She spent the next 15 minutes restating her question from multiple angles. "What happens if I leave Balad before my commander finds out?" or "What if my boyfriend files for divorce?" and "What if I resign my commission?"

I had little patience for her word games, but when I finally remembered that I had promised to make some inquiries, I picked up the phone and muted the football commentary. Peoples gave me the mildly annoyed look my garbage collector gives me when I forget to place my cans curbside and beg him to return for the pick up. This was a look I'd learned to ignore. I punched the phone number for Captain Jeff Manson and a moment later heard him spitfiring the military phone script.

"Office of the Judge Advocate (JAG). This is a non-secure line. Can I help you, sir or ma'am?" Manson was a Mormon who had befriended a few chaplains in his short career and he was used to them asking equivocal questions like, "If I knew a person who did such-and-such, could he get in trouble?"

I reworded Anderson's question, and heard Manson's best dramatic pause. He knew I was too smart for such dumb questions, but he dutifully answered with lawyerly deadpan logic and reminded me that General Order No. 1 forbids sexual contact in a warzone.

"Uh-uh, right. Yes, of course. I know that." My eyes did a barrel roll and then I changed the phone to the other ear hoping to make some sense out of the muffled hospital public address announcement I heard seeping through our closed door.

I put a hand over the phone's mouthpiece and exaggerated a whispered order to Peoples. "Open the door and see what's up."

Peoples pinged me with a look that asked, "Do I really have to get up, sir?"

I returned to my phone conversation.

"It is a court-martial offense and punishable under the Uniform Code of Military Justice, the UCMJ," Manson continued. His droning tone always reminded of my high school algebra teacher. "Furthermore, our commander has constantly declared that people who commit crimes during their deployment will be incarcerated in Balad for the duration of their sentence."

Just as Manson concluded with, "Your person or persons unnamed is looking at a six-month incarceration in our base brig," Peoples opened the door and we all heard the words, "Trauma Call, Trauma Call."

It took a few minutes for Peoples and me to register the meaning of the announcement, but the colleagues scrambling past our office knew exactly what to do. Every medical discipline poured from every nook, scrambling for their assigned places behind the red line of the ER nursing station. Hospital work had been quiet for the last few weeks and the parading blur of colorful scrubs told me that people were ready to go back to work.

"Chaplain, now," Peoples said. I loved it when he found his radio voice. No, not so much really.

"Gotta go, Captain." I said. We're getting a trauma call." The JAG voiced no objection.

My chaplain assistant bolted from our office with a speed I'd not seen from the Buckeye sanitary engineer. I caught up with him outside the ER and laid a slowing hand on his shoulder blade intended to suggest an entrance stride somewhere between panic and pretense.

Inside the doors, Dr. Deavers was summoning staff members across the red line like he was choosing sides for basketball. The ER pulsed with techno-banter, while white-coated people ordered quick assessments and sent "stat" orders for blood tests to their waiting counterparts. The tone assumed the calculated pace of an operating room more than the trauma and drama of the Hollywood ERs.

The muffled whop-whop-whop of the departing medevac helicopter momentarily shook Peoples out of his newbie glaze and sent him scrambling into the covey of people using the ER phone bank behind the nurses' station. When he found an open phone line, he called Chaplain Hearts to report our team's first trauma response. Our boss had requested to be called because he knew the political topology of our sensitive ground and he wanted to assess us. More to the point, he wanted to vet us. A few minutes later, Hearts perched on the red line with the cross-armed stance entitled to his rank as "Bird Colonel."

Even those keeping their distance like Hearts could see that our patient, 24-year-old Sergeant Justin Burton, was a cacophony of disfigurement, a tangled wreck of burned and shredded skin. His face appeared drenched with acid and a left eyeball hung from its socket like it had sprung from a children's Halloween mask. An IED blast had ripped off his right arm and skin trailed from his side like that of a shedding reptile. His open wounds boiled with a breath-stopping waft that made me wonder if my boss noticed his new chaplain holding his breath. A few minutes later, a pale Hearts answered my unspoken question when he tapped his chest and threw a thumb over his shoulder to indicate he was going outside for air.

At that moment, one of the EMTs approached me–a harried woman in her mid-thirties and she was carrying a bag. "Chaplain, please let the team know I have the patient's arm with his wedding ring." With that remark, she took off toward the morgue. I wanted to go wherever the hell Hearts had just gone.

Inside the open curtain of Trauma Bay No.1, the Trauma Czar clicked on a flashlight and waved it back and forth into Burton's only good eye. His only good pupil was blown, fixed and dilated. It was a sure sign he was gone.

"Burton! Burton!" Deavers called out like Jesus summoning the dead Lazarus from his tomb. No response. He rolled a spiked wheel across the sergeant's forehead and then onto his foot until the doc was sure the soldier was unresponsive and no longer home.

"Get Smith from the lounge!" he bellowed over his shoulder to the unit secretary.

If Deavers was our coach, then Dr. Carrie Smith was our special teams coach on call 24/7 to bring the extraordinary play action. The 5'5" athletically shaped Lieutenant Colonel was a Pennsylvania Army neurosurgeon, a freckle-faced redhead who flew solo in her specialty. The doc arrived as she did on most days, wearing a sardonic smile outlined in dark lipstick and wearing her trademark dark-colored scrub. She stepped into the curtained area, consulted Deavers, and then swiveled her attention to Burton, repeating a few tests. Finally she pulled some tweezers from her medical holster and pinched something the size of a large gumball from Burton's blackened face. Holding it at arm's length, she turned toward her surrounding colleagues and proclaimed her faith.

"Jee-zuss Kerr-ist! Did anyone notice this?" she asked. "These are his brains! He was dead before he got here. There was nothing we could have done. He's gone." She snapped off her gloves with a ferocity that seconded her own opinion. Schmidt didn't like being consulted for the obvious, anymore than I'd liked fielding evasive questions from the photogenic Nurse Anderson.

"Chaplain!" Smith called.

"Here, ma'am," I said. I felt like the kicker summoned after a bad third down.

"I imagine you'll have something to do here," she whispered. A few minutes before this, she'd been in charge, but now she didn't care to play, so she returned to the bench in the doctor's lounge.

That was okay because the three volunteers who stayed seemed like they were God's choice for what came next. Burton's giant, weeping squad leader stood beside me at what remained of Burton's right shoulder. Nurse Anderson and Sergeant Jennifer Watson placed their sympathetic hands on the soldier's thighs. Watson, a redheaded administrative assistant, was the opposite twin of Smith. She was an army paper-pusher in the eyes of some, but in the six months she'd been in Balad she'd held the hand of each dying soldier, sitting with them until the end, no matter the hour.

"I talk to them," she told me one day, "thanking them for what they have done, telling them they are a hero, and that they will never be forgotten." At first, her words sounded scripted, but many of us in Balad were anxious for death to follow a script. And who was I or anyone else to tell her she was wrong?

For a few minutes, we waited and prayed in our own way, each determined not to meet the watering eyes of another staff member. None of us had ever met the soldier, but he was each of us. The military trains you to "Never leave a fallen soldier." But who was leaving whom today?

World religions debate the time a person's soul leaves their body. I don't have any desire to weigh in on that argument, but there have been enough recorded near-death experiences to suggest that a person has some awareness of their surroundings during the moments between life and death. With that belief, I cleared my throat and addressed my remarks to the soldier.

"Justin," I called. I was breaking military protocol by using his Christian name. "Hey, man, you've got a lot of friends here. You aren't alone."

I continued talking to him but was looking at Sgt. Watson. Her eyes took me in, giving me some assurance that I was saying the right things.

"I hope you know we did the best we could to help you. Everyone did–your squad, your medic, and everyone here at the hospital. Take your leave now."

With my good-bye, I added a short prayer that permitted the staff to return to work, many of them just looking for a place to be alone. I was trying to find my space when the hospital commander pulled me aside and asked me to assemble a "Patriot Detail."

Our hospital commander was Colonel Mark Miller. At 45-years-old, Miller was a well-loved commander and surgeon that stood about 5'4" and was well renowned for his religious gym workouts that left his young subordinates huffing, hands on knees, and spent on the gym floor. Miller reminded me of his preference that the detail should be like a brief graveside service, a 15-minute eulogy of the soldier's sacrifice with a concluding prayer.

In preparation, Sgt. Watson took a quilt sent by Grandmothers for Peace to comfort "Any Soldier" and placed it over Burton's body, tucking the edges under his chin like swaddling a baby. Hospital clerical staff sent emails and dispersed word-of-mouth invitations for "all-hands-available" to assemble in our vacated trauma bay for a moment of impromptu grieving. A half dozen staff swapped their colorful hospital scrubs for a real uniform, forming a makeshift color guard.

Thirty minutes later, I took my place in the center of the wide-open emergency room facing nearly a hundred staff members who stretched along the bay's perimeter. I recognized a few faces as the young tech-school graduates who'd deplaned with me a few weeks earlier, so I knew they had never seen this level of sudden death. I also knew that many of the experienced faces in the crowd were going home on the next plane after having discovered that their exposure to so much sudden death was a breeding ground for PTSD.

The improvised mourners stood soldierly quiet, as if waiting for permission to breathe. If they were expecting me to grant them that permission, they'd keep waiting. I was feeling overcome by a self-imposed demand to make sense of it all. The crack in my soul had deflated all my pastoral wisdom and I had no theological anesthesia for their pain. I felt like a little boy digging through his pockets for candy money only to find a newly ripped hole that had drained his resources. I closed my eyes for a moment and silently begged God to let my fears pass.

They didn't pass, but they subsided a bit as I remembered an old supervisor who was fond of quoting Carl Jung, saying that it is the chaplain's "own hurt that gives a measure of his power to heal." This could have been my own death, so what would I want said? From a tight throat, I finally choked something out.

"Staff Sergeant Justin Burton was one of us. In fact, we are also him. We didn't know him, but we are less without him today. I believe he knows our presence now as he is now known by God."

I closed the ceremony with scripture and a prayer, but I remember wondering how this could possibly be all I had to offer. How could it be enough? But it had to be. It was all I had.

Peoples barked, "Ah-ten-SHUN!" His bass volume nearly caused me to stumble, but it was my cue to give the color guard the permissive nod to march toward the gurney. Their cadence was off sync and their alignment a bit curved, but their nerve was steady. They assembled around the body, unfolded the American flag and snapped its corners tight, levitating it over Burton and then releasing it until it shaped the body with a red-white-and blue silhouette. Behind the nurses' station, someone fussed with the CD player controls, and we all gave Burton a salute to the tune of Taps. I then joined the honor guard as they rolled the body from the bay. When the door closed behind us, I heard the commander encouraging everyone to go back to the work of saving lives. It was the proverbial face-slap pushing us to get on with our day. I think it was still Saturday.

We rolled the gurney outside along the wooden pallets that were laid to construct an elevated sidewalk through the parking lot gravel. A few little brown birds fought for food along the path, a backing delivery truck was beeping irreverently, and bold jets were screaming overhead. Nothing outside seemed to have any idea that someone had died inside. We pushed the gurney 20 yards, made a right turn, and stopped at the padlocked refer. Someone scrambled to unlock the double doors, and we pushed the gurney into an icy box not much bigger than a walk-in closet. When we turned to leave the frigid carton, I noticed Peoples standing outside on the boarded porch with the posed expression of a boy who was double-dog-daring himself to go inside a haunted house. Disposal was his business in Ohio, but the disposal of human remains was a new piece of emotional real estate.

After stepping from the refer, several of us remained outside to defrost in the warming afternoon. We were trading awkward glances that echoed "what the hell's next?" when a Special Forces medic emerged from a nearby food cooler.

"Hey, Chaplain. One more thing," he said. He was limping toward us on the walkway with a one-handed carry of a case of "Near Beer," a product as close to alcohol as we could get in the combat theater.

"That was a nice service, but we missed something. Would you like to help me toast this soldier's life?" the medic said, more telling than asking. He was young, but age had found his eyes.

We answered with accenting nods, and he threw a can to each of us. The cold aluminum on my sweating hands gave me a chill.

"None of us knew him, but we can still toast a fellow soldier," he said, and we simultaneously popped the lids. The bursting sound reminded me of the synchronized breaking of communion wafers during worship. The sacred snap sometimes echoes under the right conditions. Even though I'd never finished a beer in my life, I'd certainly not been anywhere more sacred than where we stood on that pallet.

"The first sip is for Burton," he declared.

"Burton!" we said.

Then the unshaven medic coaxed us to raise our cans above our head.

"We spill the beer the way Burton spilled his blood," he said. The moment had all the liturgy of a Sunday Mass. The last part of the ceremony called for us to turn the cans on their side until several ounces muddied the dirt. Then we settled the cans just below our beltline until the medic raised his can again, and said, "To you. You are my brothers."

His words reminded me of a priest raising the wine chalice and quoting Jesus: "This is my blood which was spilled for you."

The only thing I knew for sure at that point was that it was going to be hard to find grace and salvation in that place and I couldn't help but wonder if Nurse Anderson already knew that.

CHAPTER 6

TRIALS AND SMILES

A week after pouring Near Beer into the dirt I lost my way again. This time it was more literally than figuratively. It happened while walking the gravel path from my hooch to the hospital to prepare for the Protestant worship service. Instead of following the western path to the medical compound, I made an errant northern arch along the fence of the busiest aerial port in the world.

When I realized my mistake, I stopped to plot a corrective route when a sound resembling the opening of a high-pressure hose disrupted my concentration. The gush began softly but suggested a coming crescendo that wouldn't be muted in the early morning dust storm. I stopped, planted my size 12 boots in the rocky road, and clamped my hands around oversized ears. Nearby, an F-16 fighter jet thundered off the runway to begin its hourly defensive tactical pattern called Combat Air Patrol (CAP). If Balad had been a high school campus, the jet pilots would have been the jocks spinning donuts around the parking lot in rust-colored El Caminos. I waited until the plane disappeared through a pinprick in the clouds and lowered my hands in time to see an NCO walking toward me like he had a secret to tell. He loaded a smile on his broad face and locked his eyes with mine, finding just the right moment to release a smart-alecky missile from his crisp salute: "What's the matter, Chaplain? Don't you like the sound of freedom?"

With that well-timed military cliché, he resumed a cocky cadence that suggested he might be late for his early morning publicity shoot.

"Love it, Chief," I called after him, but under my breath, I muttered, "Whose freedom?" I mumbled.

The mission of Balad remained loud and clear but mostly loud. Fly. Fly through the heat. Fly through the night. Fly to fight. Fly unless you fry. Fly in order to protect the oil we needed to do the same damn thing tomorrow. Thus the genesis of the well-worn joke: "Groundhog Day, again!"

I suppose I felt somewhat safer watching the circling F-16, so I stopped a moment to clutch the airfield fence and consider what might be going on inside a distant Quonset hut covered with camouflage netting. The concealment did little to hide what everyone knew. The hut nested military drones of prey called Global Hawks, MQ-1 Predators, and MQ-9 Reapers. Pilots flew the planes remotely from Riverside, California, where they sat in dark rooms and shadowed suspected insurgents for days. Five hundred miles north of Riverside, my Sacramento Intelligence squadron hunched over computer screens working to confirm hostile targets. Finally, a potbellied Air Force colonel in Las Vegas issued a kill order and the insurgent ran out of luck. The clinical operation sought to get "them" before "they" got us.

Cameras mounted on nearby buildings watched me watching ground crews reload the seven-barrel Gatling guns on the A-10 Warthogs with enough ammunition to fill every square inch of football field-sized targets. In glaring contrast to these killer bats, Medevac helicopters took fuel from T-shirted maintenance crews. These were the birds we used to respond when bullets and IED shrapnel flew in our direction.

I loosened my grip on the fence and turned to a recognizable path toward the hospital compound. A few minutes later, I walked through the maze of blast walls where Kenyan guards at a desk similar to one staffed by gray-hairs at my pediatric hospital cleared me for entry. With a few twists in the hallway, I found my place in the hospital chapel, a 15-by-20-foot colorless room with cement walls and a single window that, if it had been operable, would have opened into the false wall behind it. It sat on the ground floor just above Saddam's old torture chamber. The violent history echoed through our hospital walls issuing a chilling demand that we distill a better purpose for our building.

Inside, I caught Peoples proudly primping with the newly installed 32-inch computer monitor he'd requisitioned to project my sermon notes. I wasn't late for worship, but I was late enough that Peoples greeted me with a question mark in his salutation.

"Morning, sir," he said. He added a calculated slant on his left eyebrow.

"Good morning, Staff Sergeant Peoples," I said. My tone was intended to be a humorous reminder that the definition of "late" was anyone who arrived after the officer.

It was a few hours before our 10:00 a.m. service and Peoples was fussing with the altar flowers as if arranging them for a visiting Pope. He adorned the altar with properly colored cloths, lit candles, and arranged the folding chairs, loading them with bibles.

"How many communion cups should I pour, Sir?"

"25."

"Really?" he said. We'd seen less than 15 congregants on our first two Sundays, and I suppose he didn't want me getting any illusions of grandeur.

"Where's your faith, Sergeant?"

Instead of answering, he started riffling through his desk drawers as if his faith was in one of them.

"This time we're doing communion a bit differently," I said.

He kept shuffling his desk drawers without bothering to look at me, but I continued talking.

"I need you to fill five cups with white wine and place them in the center of the communion tray surrounded by cups of purple grape juice."

"Don't that kinda go against General Order No. 1?" he asked. He accented his question with a smartass chuckle, but he knew that the order prohibiting alcohol made allowances for religious services. In fact, I occasionally cajoled our congregation by telling them that they enjoyed the only bar in town.

"You going to make the night shift do this, too?" he asked. His question nearly broke in two with snickering guffaws.

"Not yet."

"Right," he said.

Peoples didn't much like doing things differently, but he respected my effort to accommodate congregants ranging from teatotaling Southern Baptists to stein-grabbing Lutherans. Nevertheless, we both knew that our night shift colleague frowned on such accommodations. He was very much like my father, a Southern Baptist pastor who followed the direction of the Baptist Covenant that admonished followers to "abstain from the sale and use of intoxicating drinks."

My sixth grade Sunday school teacher backed my father's view by asserting that Jesus never actually turned water into wine. "Actually," she said, "Jesus transformed the bad wine into the most excellent version of Welch's Grape Juice." With that explanation, most of us cocked our heads like my dog whining during my trumpet rehearsals.

When Peoples finally found the corkscrew in a bottom desk drawer, he popped the cork on our government issued booze and gave it a socialite whiff. "Wonderful bouquet."

I took the bottle from him and inhaled, adding "2009 is a very good year."

Peoples thought for a moment and said, "I suppose you're going to have to explain why we are using the Catholic wine today."

"Because why?" I asked.

"We are out of our white wine," he said.

"And that makes a difference, how?"

He huffed at my ignorance. "It's the same color as the purple grape juice and I don't think you want any mistakes."

"Oh."

Peoples raised the bottle at arm's length and filled five thimble-sized cups with purple wine and 20 surrounding cups with purple Welch's juice. He lit the candles, spread the wrinkles from the altar cloth with his broad hands, and replaced the Crucifix from the early morning Catholic service with the non-Jesus Protestant cross.

Everything came into place by 9:45 a.m., and Peoples fiddled with his new sound system so it would play the religious version of elevator music. In good evangelical fashion, we posted ourselves in the chapel doorway to welcome new arrivals, trading their smiles for our bulletins. They came one-by-one, and sometimes two-by-two, but no matter their pairing, they carried bibles and guns. The Geneva Convention, our bible when it comes to ethically killing people, forbids chaplains to carry guns, but medics can use lethal force to protect their wounded. Thus, I shook the hand of the first morning congregant, a petite nurse whose M9 Beretta seemed to cover her entire hip.

"Welcome," I said.

She looked down, thanked her shoes, and found a seat. After her, came an unshaven soldier who sidestepped me.

"How are you?" I asked. He didn't hear me because he was fumbling to cram his M-16 under our folding-chair pews.

At 1000 hours, I found my place behind the lectern and furtively counted two-dozen staff members dressed in multicolored scrubs like Joseph and his dream coat. At 1001 hours, three ambulatory patients pushed IV stands with bags into the back row and took the last seats. I recognized them as the Marines who had rolled their Humvee earlier in the week. I shot Peoples my best I-told-you-so smirk, reconfigured my face for worship mode, and opened my Bible to read a scripture and give our invocation.

Just as I said "amen," I looked up to note how many guns were in the house. I have no affinity for guns, but I suppose you shouldn't go to war without them.

"My, my. I hope you like my sermon today."

The remark got me a few laughs before I called Captain Sara Schaefer to the lectern to begin our congregational singing. Sara was a tall, pear-shaped woman in her late thirties who struggled to pass her fitness test. She preceded me to Balad by a few months and rediscovered church after watching too many patients die.

She pressed the remote control and brought our first song to the widescreen that Peoples had installed, "This is the Day That the Lord has Made."

"Let's sing all verses," she said. I groaned a bit. I really hate that song, but it seems to be one of the few that our congregants had memorized.

I don't think Sara heard me groan because she started the song with a smile, waving her right hand to hold our beat. She sang toward the ceiling, but all the while she kept a hand on her belt-mounted pager. She wanted to be ready should she be recalled to the ICU ward to disconnect life support from a brain-dead Iraqi girl.

She followed the first song with a contemporary arrangement of Amazing Grace, but no matter what the style, it is a moving song in a deployed location. Afterward, Sara paused to double check the order of service. She cleared her throat and managed a barely audible summons. "Your turn, Chaplain."

I grabbed the corded microphone and explained that our new arrangement of grape juice and wine was designed to give them a choice that accommodated all Protestant traditions. Most of them nodded dutifully and I cued the ever-present Peoples with a lift of my brow to take his place beside me. While he presented the communion trays from bent elbows, I raised my palms from waist to chest to signal the parishioners to form a single-file line through the tight center of the 24-seat room.

Each congregant shuffled to the front and made their choice from Peoples' trays. My litany was simple. When they took a wafer, I said, "His body, broken for you." When they chose their communion cup, I said, "His blood, spilled for you."

It seemed easy enough. I was sure we were coping well with the communion change. I'd been worried for nothing. Actually, I'd been worried for the wrong reason. It turned out that it wasn't the wine or the guns that I found most intimidating. It was the tears that my parishioners were hiding from one another.

I first noticed the tears when a phlebotomist arrived at the communion altar holding a makeup-stained tissue with her hymnbook pages wet with pain. I'd noticed her as she bookmarked the hymnal with her stares. She seemed to have finished Amazing Grace in a waffling tone, amazed at her own emptiness and how easily grace could be spent.

The clumsy soldier, who had earlier fumbled with his weapon, followed her to the altar while wiping his face with his camouflaged sleeve. I secretly hoped maybe these were tears of joy to celebrate the end of his thirteen-month tour, but I knew he was likely grieving the friend he'd lost. Whatever the reasons, the tears marked the contrast between the past joys and present despair.

We all had our fair share of tears, but it was nearly impossible to distinguish their etymology. Some tears were likely shed for the 28-year-old Iraqi translator who had been obliterated so badly by an IED that we immediately and unceremoniously stored his remains in the morgue. Possibly we were crying for the 22-year-old newlywed soldier who had died in a rollover during his first week. Or maybe, tears were simply an emotional relief to the three soldiers who amazingly survived the same incident with minimal injuries.

The grief contagion spread and my voice cracked during my last few litanies as I found it harder to swallow. I was trying to uphold the podium-look that chaplains are taught to maintain. "Never let them see you get emotional in the pulpit," was the constant advice from my eighty-year-old seminary professor Dr. J.P. Allan. "Swallow your emotion or use them for a dramatic pause, because no one trusts a weepy preacher."

While the last of the congregants took their communion, I realized I was straining to hold back my own tears for several reasons. I'd slept hesitantly those first few weeks. Like most of our medical staff, I constantly checked my pager during the night to see if I missed a midnight mass-casualty call. Sometimes the thud of a distant mortar sent me snuggling with my flak vest. But mostly, after nearly 30 years of sleeping with the same woman, it was difficult to find satisfying bunk space under a scratchy wool blanket. When I finally slept, early morning dreams taunted me into thinking that I was waking beside Becky.

When everyone returned to their seats, I ping-ponged a glance off the eyes of each congregant. For whatever reason, they'd all brought their own personal tears to the altar. I looked down at my empty hands in search of a relevant crumb of meaning to offer my parishioners. What would I say?

In the back of the room, Peoples suppressed his emotion with a self-conscious cough. His eyes said, "Get on with it, Chaplain."

"Let us pray," I said. It was the best response I knew, but not the most honest. I should have said, "I gotta pray because I don't know what else to do. I am still lost."

I cleared the excuses from my throat and found my prayer. "God, please give me strength and clarity in the fog of war that I may be able to encourage your people. Amen. Just that, for now God, Amen."

When I returned to the pulpit, I carried a new appreciation of how tears often mark the moment in which a people touch the unutterable places of their heart. That ineffable place becomes the sacred language of divine conversations and reminds me to discard superfluous issues and stay connected with the real hurts of people. This was a lesson perhaps lost for our evening shift Chaplain, Merck Johnson.

The chaplain was a young captain from the frowning tradition who spent the past four months as Chaplain Roamer's nighttime counterpart. He was a lanky blond with a shaved head and a nervous demeanor. My guess was that he'd been assigned the nightshift as a way of minimalizing his patient contact, because not even the most obnoxious chaplain would wake a sleeping patient. Since the uncompromising Johnson was scheduled to leave the following week, I decided to postpone my blended communion policy until his replacement arrived. However, I did order Peoples to clean and refill the communion trays as a parting favor to Johnson. I probably should have coordinated postponing the wine with my chaplain assistant, but as sometimes happens, God had other plans.

When Johnson arrived for our daily change-of-shift report, I briefed him about the tears and the new patient admits. He looked past me and smiled to see the communion trays apparently filled with grape juice and ready for his 8 p.m. service. Neither one of us knew that the purple cups only appeared to be grape juice. My sleepwalking assistant, still jet-lagged, inadvertently filled the trays with rosé wine.

When Peoples and I arrived the next morning for our end-of-shift report, we found the unwashed communion trays strewn across my desk. Johnson was loaded for bear, and he gave us hell, or his version of it anyway. He told us how he had preached a particularly rousing swansong and then raised a communion cup toward the congregation to cue a unified imbibing. He pronounced, as most Baptist chaplains do, "This cup represents the blood of Christ spilled for you. Take it and drink it all." Then he threw back the half-ounce content like a shot glass and coughed out a raspy question, "Is there something wrong with this juice?"

I hid my smile as I imagined bemused parishioners licking their lips and responding in chorus, "It's wine, chaplain. It's real wine."

"Today was only the second time in my life that I've had wine," he claimed. Apparently, a few of his roguish high school friends tricked him into tasting wine 20 years previous. The last time I'd seen a look like his on a Baptist face was when my mother drank some of the spiked punch at the graduation party of my church friend, Wendy Sommers. Wendy had some roguish brothers.

As I watched him pack his last few things from our shared desk, an impish smile formed in my mischievous heart. I profusely apologized while jokingly pleading to be excused.

"I'm so sorry, I think I missed the seminary lecture where we learned how to turn wine into Welch's Juice."

He wasn't amused, but he was happy with his ticket home that week. And so were most of us who practiced the "smiling tradition."

CHAPTER 7

DIGESTING THE INDIGESTIBLE

"Ready for lunch?" Peoples asked as he did nearly every day before noon.

"Kinda early, isn't it?"

"This is Wednesday," he said.

I shrugged. I wasn't worried. "Wednesdays come every week. Besides, February has three more of them." I continued typing my weekly report.

"Come on, Sir. We wanna beat the rush, don't we?"

That was our routine. After working 30 days, we'd gelled well, but when things slowed, I became *The Odd Couple*'s Felix, fixated on propriety. Peoples became the ice-cream-dribbling Oscar who swiveled in his desk chair while reading Internet conspiracies aloud.

"Surf and turf," he added.

"Isn't it the same steak, lobster, and shrimp we've had for the last four Wednesdays?"

He knew better than to answer.

"And since it's probably the same menu we'll have for the next twelve Wednesdays, you can go without me this time. I gotta finish writing my report."

"Alrighty then." He sailed into the hallway but encored a few seconds later to grab his signature goggles and scarf. "After a while," he promised. His "while" returned with a self-shaming headshake because he had forgotten his military ID. We used the ID to access our desktop computers, but he would need it to show the Kenyan guards assigned to defend our food with M16s.

Peoples loved obsessing over which one of the four cafeterias he would choose for every particular meal. Our cafeterias were called DFACs (pronounced D-fac), an ingenious acronym for Dining Facilities Administration Center. Each DFAC was the size of three gymnasiums packed with rows of heart-stopping dessert bars with artery-clogging cheesecakes illuminated in refrigerated mirrored cabinets. We often joked that the colossal cafeterias were the most dangerous places on base and that the guards were employed to restrain caloric-crazed corporals from the arsenal of stockpiled fat bombs. I usually left the DFAC slurping a Baskin-Robbins milkshake.

"This food almost makes you forget you are at war," our chief nurse said a few weeks before a "coronary event" caused him to plant his chubby face into a plate of macaroni and cheese. Fellow nurses revived the six-foot-six jolly colonel, and he was medevac'd home where he miraculously served three years of active duty prior to his retirement.

After Peoples left the building, I made a few more edits on my report before shuffling down the hospital hallway to our miniaturized DFAC. The eatery was sized like a take-out facility tucked in our front entrance, but I ate there in hopes of bypassing the gluttonous temptations of the larger dining hall. My self-limiting strategy lasted only a few days before I realized that I was eating meals that our food services people had trucked over from the larger DFAC. Nevertheless, I still liked the small dining hall for its collegial vibe.

I queued up in the food line where an acned Indonesian server, sweating over the steaming rice, asked me for my preference of fish or shrimp.

"I'll take a small portion of shrimp, please," I said, even as he slid a full plate on my tray. I added a canned Diet Pepsi and plastic utensils and followed the staff gaggle through the crowded room looking for a seat.

"Is this seat taken?" I asked a scrub-clad man sitting beside the refrigerated dessert case.

He pushed the chair out with his foot without looking up. When I tried repositioning the chair with my foot, a few shrimp swam downstream to the floor. So much for a small serving.

The stranger gave my plate a frown, and I answered with a joke.

"I'm on a diet," I said. "My goal is one pound a week."

"Really?" he asked. "You're trying to lose a pound a week?"

"No." I paused to stuff a few shrimp in my mouth. "I'm actually trying to *gain* a pound a week. I think I'm a bit ahead of my goal."

I looked around to see who heard my little standup routine, but hearing no applause, I sat down.

"Chaplain. Right?" He pointed to the embroidered cross above my left breast pocket that supported his guess.

"Yes, Sir." I nodded.

He tracked his index finger over the nametag sewn above my right breast pocket.

"Burk-es?" he guessed. It was the most common mispronunciation of my name.

"It's 'Burkes,' with one syllable, but most folks here call me 'Chap.'"

"I'm Dr. Timothy Sullivan, the new orthopedic surgeon," he said. The verbal dance began with the customary moves of "where ya from?" and "how long ya been in?"

Sullivan was a Texas Republican whose short stature kept his feet on the inside bar of his chair. He spoke with a downward gaze that kept my focus on his blond hair that receded past his reddened forehead and retreated into stubble patches over his sprouting ears.

I've met few surgeons who are conversation starters, but when they speak they usually speak in certain tones, like the fighter pilots of the medical field. They are people who fix things with little time for feeling or emotion. Even if something can't be fixed, they may still claim they have fixed it. Just as I was beginning to wish I'd gone with Peoples, the doc stirred his chili macaroni into his fruit salad and looked up.

"What do you do during your shift?" he asked.

I paused a moment, trying to find his tone. I wasn't sure whether his accent stressed "you" or "do." Was I being asked to justify my presence or regale him with miraculous stories? Maybe he was cynically asking how I found the time for lunch. I wasn't sure, so I let my mind sort through the past three days to find a straightforward approach.

"Have you met our little burn patient?" I asked. I knew he hadn't.

Sullivan shook his head while draining his Red Bull. He was listening now.

I began a story about a father who approached our front gate with his son in his arms. Our security forces forced the father to lie prone while they searched them both for explosives. With his face in the dirt, the father pleaded with the gate translator to allow the boy admission to the American hospital. This was his "only chance," the dad said. A military policeman responded to the translated pleas by requesting for doctor to triage the patient. The hospital sent our only pediatrician, Dr. Roger Williams, a slight man in his forties. Williams was a long way from his home base in San Antonio where he treated colds, broken arms, and chicken pox. He'd never been to war, and he certainly wasn't used to making house calls, much less outside the fortified gates of our base.

Williams grabbed a hospital technician and Rahim, our medical translator. The three of them suited up with battle armor and weapons, and the technician drove the trio in our hospital ambulance into the only "front" they'd ever see during their six-month deployment. They stopped just outside the tangled gate of concertina wire and massive columns of concrete laid sideways. While guards held M-16s over a little boy wrapped tightly in his father's arms, the medical team heard a story infectious with heartbreak.

"Iraqi hospitals turned this boy away," the translator repeated to Williams. "They said, 'Take your son home to die.'"

Williams found third-degree burns over fifty percent of the boy's body. "Iraqi docs were right, but he doesn't have to die in this filth," he told the translator. "Tell the father we will treat his son."

In the DFAC, Sullivan put his fork down and leaned his chair back while popping open his second RedBull. "Wow, that's so sad," he said. "But I still don't see your part."

I held up a hand as if telling a child to wait for the crossing light. "Dr. Williams asked me to see the boy and his dad a few days later."

"But, you don't …" he started to say.

"Know the language?" I said, completing his question. "Comfort can sometimes be translated."

"It's just that – and I mean no offense – but what could you do?"

I reprised my wait-for-it hand and explained that Dr. Williams had asked me to meet with Hakeem. I met them both in the boy's ICU room the next day where Williams was weaving bandages between the boy's toes and knees. The handsome eight-year-old patient had wholesome but moistened eyes. I beamed a smile toward his untouched face, but his emotional echo returned flat. At first the boy seemed perfect, but his father's eyes directed my assessment below Hakeem's waist where I saw one massive blister.

Williams spoke in whispered tones as if worried that the father might suddenly master English. "Iraqi grade schools don't teach their kids to 'stop, drop and roll.' The kid was playing with matches and cooking fuel. Bad combo."

I wasn't sure what to say to that, but murmured, "I brought something." I sounded like I wasn't sure I had brought something. Compassion isn't translated easily.

Williams tossed me a rapid glance. "Whatcha got, Chap?"

I turned toward Hakeem's father who was almost shorter than Williams and definitely less nourished. His sunken eyes projected the familiar fear I'd seen in Benton's father back in the pediatric oncology ward of my Sacramento hospital. We didn't share the language, but we shared the title of Dad, the role of *Baba.*

I reached into my satchel and withdrew a bilingual Quran. I kissed its cover and opened to a passage I'd previously found. I placed a finger on the Arabic portion coaxing the father to read, "The true servants of the merciful Lord are those who say to him: 'Make our families happy, and make us examples to all who honor you.'"

He wrapped his trembling arms around the sacred book and then pressed his chapped lips on the cover before placing it above Hakeem's head. He turned to me and brought his hand to his heart. I mimed the movement and pulled my hand to my chest as if trying to reach inside for something else to give. When Williams finished his bandaging, I removed one more thing from my satchel – a blanket from Operation Iraqi Children embroidered with Disney's Goofy. I raised the blanket above my head and unfurled it until the flop-eared dog was draped over the drab of my camouflage scrub.

Hakeem surrendered a nearly imperceptible smile and Dr. Williams nodded his permission to blanket the boy's freshly bandaged body. Again the dad and I brought our hands to our hearts as if we'd just found a place in each other where we agreed that no child should have this pain.

I took a pause in my lunchtime story and checked my watch. The cafeteria was clearing out.

"Did that happen last week?" asked my new surgeon friend.

"Yup."

"How's Hakeem doing today?"

I shook my head. I had just enough time to tell him about the previous morning. I had been sitting in my office with Peoples when our Chief of Staff, Erica Stanton, stuck her head into our small space and shouted, "Ethics Committee meeting in ten minutes."

Peoples shot me a questioning look. "That ain't good," he said. He was learning.

When all the participants were seated, Stanton took the lead chair. She was about 98 pounds, but the bird colonel insignia on her collar added a ton. Her eyes could grab you like a tractor beam, and when she was done with you, you agreed with her or you were done. But in our meeting, she exposed a different side.

"Our little burn patient isn't doing so well," she said. "The only question before us today is: Where are we going to let him die?"

Stanton explained that Hakeem had become septic from the infected burns and he'd had a stroke. Committee members were visibly shaken but didn't move. In the states, Hakeem would be placed with pediatric hospice, but the lack of sterility in Iraq made placement problematic. Stanton's chair squeaked as she panned the room waiting for any one of the half dozen members to offer advice.

I allowed an involuntary stutter and suddenly all eyes were on me. Stanton nodded for me to speak.

"I know we were all looking for a miracle here, but I wonder what that miracle might look like if we shift our expectations of what *miracle* means. Maybe the true miracle won't be Hakeem's survival, but it will be the moment when his family sees that Christians honor the life of a Muslim child and share the pain of his death."

More chairs squeaked.

"Perhaps the true miracle here isn't about saving what we have, but about fully appreciating what remains. Maybe the true miracle won't always be about saving the world, but about gaining new appreciation for a piece of it."

This part of my story had my lunch mate listening for more.

"What did they say?" he asked.

"There was more discussion, but 20 minutes later they unanimously recommended that Hakeem be allowed to die at home on the strongest possible pain relief."

"Home? You mean?"

'Yes, whatever hovel they called home," I said. "It may not be clean, but it was the loving option."

The surgeon lost all interest in his meal, so I finished my story by describing how I'd found Dr. Williams readying the boy for his homecoming that afternoon. Williams taught Hakeem's father how to rewrap the burns. Culturally, the nursing role was a "feminine" one, but the father bucked his traditions and seemed to love Hakeem more than our reckless war gave anyone the right to do.

When the bandaging lesson was completed, none of us wanted to face what came next. Nurses pretended to be reading charts and technicians took meaningless measurements. Sniffles restrained the emotion no one could afford to expend. Finally, Dr. Williams placed Hakeem into the same strong paternal arms that had brought him to us, and our translator escorted them from the unit, leaving a torrent of staff tears in his wake.

For a few more minutes, Dr. Sullivan and I just sat in the DFAC digesting the story. Food service workers cleared lunch dishes around us. Overhead, jets screamed above the whop-whop-whop of incoming helicopters.

Dr. Sullivan cleared his throat and shifted his line of questioning.

"Where do you get the strength to do all that?" His eyes reflected maybe a trace of moisture.

I glanced toward our greasy ceiling and simply said, "From the same place we all get it."

I paused.

"I do what I also hope you do," I told him. "In the midst of chaos, I pray. I share a laugh. I wipe a tear. I offer a shoulder. I lend an ear. And at the end of the day – whether quiet or rushed – I strive to be a visible reminder of the holy in a place that desperately needs it."

Just about then, we heard the PA speakers vibrate: "Trauma call. Trauma call. Trauma call times four." The surgeon leaned forward in his chair and fired his last questions at me over the condiments.

"Don't tell me you go for those, too?"

"Yup," I said and grabbed my satchel.

"What do you do in the middle of that crazy mess?" He knew our trauma calls could resemble the inside of a frenzied session at the New York Stock Exchange.

"Sorry, got to go. I'll have to get back to you on that one."

CHAPTER 8

ENEMIES NEED PRAYER AND CARE TOO

As February hinted at March, I learned to grab my rest whenever and wherever I found it. My best downtime came on Wednesday afternoons when a few of our parish chaplains voluntarily surrendered half of their day off to relieve me. The extra help meant I could take a long lunch and a short nap in my hooch. On the last Wednesday afternoon in the month, I had just settled into my bunk when the late season rain began pounding my metal roof. I burrowed into my covers and succumbed to the hypnotic rhythm of the shattering drops.

I woke to find the rain had stopped, but the rainy season had begun with an intensity that sought compensation for its off-season tardiness. The problem was water has no place to go in a desert. An hour of rain could bring a week of troubles and the simplest things like fueling our generators and siphoning our porta-potties became arduous tasks that doubled in length. I sloshed to the hospital through a fudge-like landscape layered with mousse and swimming with chocolate milk. With each step, my boots slurped up the gunk and added an extra pound to each foot.

Not far from the hospital, a two-striped airman offered me a salute as he stood atop a patch of dry gravel outside the hospital.

"This mud sucks, Chaplain!" she said.

"Embrace the suck," I said, returning her salute.

A few minutes later, I stood in the hospital foyer dealing with the suck of my mud-caked rubber boots and apologizing to the TCNs who were mopping an endless loop of hospital hallways.

"Sorry. Sorry for the mess," I kept telling our Filipino orderly. He was wiping mud from the walls slung there by careless airmen like myself who had hurriedly removed their boots. The deference in his glance rebuffed my apologies.

"It's okay, Sir. No worries. No to worry, Sir." he said.

I carried my muddied boots to my office in my stocking feet and placed them on my outside porch. I had just propped my white-socked feet on my desk when Peoples came strolling in.

"My, you look comfy," he said.

"Yup." I think he recognized the screw-you tone of my reply. He shook his finger at my unauthorized white socks and started to say something, but the intercom announcement squawked over his words.

"Trauma call. Trauma call. Trauma call times two."

I jumped into the clean zip-up boots I kept under my desk and once again joined the cavalcade of speed walkers in the hallway. When we arrived at the ER, we took our place just behind the red line and waited for the first patient to arrive in Trauma Bay 1. Within ninety seconds, three orderlies staggered through the double doors with the first gurney. Their patient was over six-and-a-half feet long and he overlapped the edges of the gurney. The soldier's size forced the volunteers to make slow pivots to minimize the turning momentum.

Once inside the curtained area, technicians connected tubing and IVs from an array of high-tech plugs along the wall. Our Trauma Czar, Dr. Deavers, stepped up and shone his flashlight into the fading eyes of Army Staff Sgt. Mark Bellhart. He quickly made his initial assessment.

Our 32-year-old patient from Quakertown, Pennsylvania, had a bullet lodged in his balding forehead. Everyone stood quiet as they awaited the prognosis. Most stateside physicians would designate our patient as "expectant." They would initiate comfort measures to prepare the family for the inevitable and move to the next patient. But not our doc. Not our hospital.

"Call neuro!" Deavers said.

Deavers wasn't ready to call it a day. I couldn't help but feel that it didn't take a brain surgeon to realize Bellhart was an inert mass of torn clothing and lost hopes. But apparently it did.

While waited for neurology, a team of armed soldiers slap-opened the rear ER doors and wheeled in an unidentified Iraqi strapped to a gurney. Our team accepted the cart and matched it with Trauma Bay 8. One of the soldiers, tall and tanned, introduced the patient as an "insurgent piece of dung."

In contrast to Bellhart, the insurgent was shrinking and dark, unwashed and unshaven. He wore the torn khaki pants of a farm hand and the new one-handed Combat Application Tourniquet (CAT) above his right knee. The bandage is indispensable in combat for stopping the arterial blood flow to an extremity, but we wondered who had wasted it on the enemy.

There was no time to hear that question answered. A minute later, our neurosurgeon, Dr. Smith, appeared out of nowhere, and Peoples and I focused on her.

Smith cautiously peeled back Bellhart's head bandages, pursing her lips and humming as she searched for an exit wound in the caked blood of a receding hairline. She pricked his finger with a surgical instrument hoping she'd see signs that Bellhart could feel pain. Nothing. She didn't find an exit, but she did find her anger.

"Prep him!" she suddenly ordered. "He's got no chance in hell, but I'm going to try something."

Both Smith and Deavers knew they were risking an outcome most of us considered worse than death. They were risking that Bellhart would live out his life on a machine and most soldiers would rather die than face that. Nevertheless, our team made daily incursions into the realm of the impossible. We risked those kinds of outcomes because we wanted to give families a chance to say goodbye to their soldier in the American hospital in Germany. Most soldiers considered this final reunification with family to be priceless.

The staff wheeled their patient into the operating room, but I returned to my office to wait for a call I guesstimated would come a few hours after surgery. Peoples wasn't so sure of that timing, so he positioned himself outside the OR where he could peer through the operating room's glass window and relay word back to me. From there, he watched Smith as she took only five minutes prep time before pushing a scalpel through Bellhart's scalp to stop the bleeding. At first she had difficulty finding the bullet because it had fragmented and plummeted into Bellhart's brain, leaving behind a trail of gray matter. However, when she found the bullet, Peoples heard her say what she had instinctively known.

"Damn it. I can't stop this bleeding!" She looked up to tell the startled Peoples, "Get the chaplain." A few minutes later, Peoples came huffing though our office door. "They... they ... they, want you in the OR! Now!"

"What? Why? What the hell am I supposed to do in surgery?" *Did I say that out loud?* I rephrased my question. "Do you mean actually 'inside' the surgical suite?"

"I don't know, but you better get over there fast."

In my previous ten years as a civilian hospital chaplain, I'd never responded directly to the OR. Why now? My only hope was that Peoples was a doofus who got the request wrong. I reloaded my boots with reluctant feet and walked down the hall to the OR.

My worship-leading nurse, Sara, met me outside the OR. Her gown was blood streaked in long lines of deep reds.

"They need you in there, Chaplain," she said.

"Need" seemed like such a strong word for requesting a layperson like myself, but I knew the OR staff to be a superstitious lot who sometimes imagined chaplains had the ability to conjure and cajole the divine. My response to their magical thinking was to help them understand that God was already there and needn't be fabricated.

I donned a mask, gown, and gloves, and pushed through the swinging doors where I was overwhelmed by the remnants of their daring effort. Tubes, IVs, bags of blood, bandages, and pharmacological equipment and monitors lay strewn about the room, and the rusty smell of blood was impermeable to dismissal. The staff paced the room, leaving blood-splashed footprints that traced the sacred struggle for life. I didn't have to bring God to the OR; God had arrived long before and his footprints were everywhere to prove it.

Smith gave me the perfunctory nod to proceed, so I turned my attention to the patient where I saw something I will never forget. Blood was pouring from Bellhart's head as if from a bathroom faucet my kid had left running, puddled on the floor, forging inlets along the uneven tile. For a moment I held my breath, but Deavers resuscitated me from my breathlessness with a request.

"Chap! Our boy isn't going to make it. Can you say a few words?"

I breathed again and found my prayer zone. My prayer became a short effort to reach a grieving staff.

"God, thank you for these incredible heroes who struggled today to save the life of another hero. God, we need an extra helping of courage now, but not the kind of courage fabricated for presentations and ceremony. We need a sustaining courage that will help us do our job despite the failure we may be feeling right now."

After my "amen," I raised my head and felt disappointment saturating the room. Our statistics had dropped a tick.

I later learned from a news clipping that Bellhart's family was notified in their Pennsylvania home by a team who had the same unfortunate timing I'd had years earlier – they interrupted the birthday party for a six-year-old girl with the news that her father was dead. Bellhart's wife told the team her husband had volunteered for his second tour in hopes of helping the young and less-experienced soldiers in his unit.

The team commander assured Bellhart's wife that her husband was in the process of helping those young soldiers when he responded to an IED attack in the town of Mushadah. Outside the town, Bellhart took control of his unit while under enemy fire, but was felled by a sniper's bullet through his helmet. Those actions earned him a Purple Heart, a Bronze Star, and more than a half-dozen other medals.

A moment after my prayer, someone broke the silence and suggested that I should pray for the other guy. The staff saw my puzzled look above my surgical mask, so someone added, "Pray that the doctors won't get court-martialed for killing the bastard."

The staff knew what I was only just then learning. The patient in the adjoining OR was the man who'd come to our ER with the combat tourniquet on his leg. He was the one who likely killed Bellhart and was now receiving world-class medical care from the same people who were grieving Bellhart's loss.

I ignored the sarcasm in the request and took it like the challenge an athlete feels to beat his personal best. I was great at praying for our soldiers, but could I pray for the enemy, too? If so, would the prayer be real? You learn a lot when you care for your friends, but you learn a great deal more when you care for your enemies.

I released the prayer where I stood. "God, help the doctors to do the right thing. Amen."

There was little feeling to my prayer, but it was my best effort to live the words Jesus taught in the Sermon on the Mount: "You're familiar with the old written law, 'Love your friend,' and its unwritten companion, 'hate your enemy'? I'm challenging that," Jesus flatly stated. "I'm telling you to love your enemies.... If all you do is love the lovable, do you expect a bonus? Anybody can do that. If you simply say hello to those who greet you, do you expect a medal? Any run-of-the-mill sinner does that" (*The Message*, Matthew 5.43-44a, 47).

Our trauma team didn't settle for "run-of-the-mill." They were applauded for their efforts to save Bellhart, but their efforts to save the shooter's leg didn't go over well with everyone in our hospital. There was talk, the kind of bravado that people use to fantasize revenge. Talk like, "I'd like to put my finger deep into his wound" or "I'd like to put a bullet in his head." Truth is, I may have felt some of those things myself. When the vengeful thoughts faded, a few of us started wondering who it was that so skillfully applied the life-saving tourniquet. We had our answer the next day.

While making my change-of-shifts rounds, I came across members of Bellhart's unit in our patient administration office as they made plans to transfer him home. One of the members, a 6-foot-three Pennsylvania medic in a sun-bleached uniform, explained how he tried to stop Bellhart's bleeding. Like me, he was overwhelmed by how much blood he saw and was second-guessing his actions. Doctors assured him that he'd done all that was possible and that even the surgeon couldn't stop that kind of bleeding.

The medic thanked us for the information and then nonchalantly added, "Stopping the shooter's bleeding was easy with the new CAT." His comparison stopped the chatter in the room as we struggled to fully comprehend his words. Was he saying that he saved the life of the man who killed his squad member? He was.

We exchanged expressions that said we'd expect our buddies to kill the SOB, not save him. Put an M9 to his head and pull the trigger. Yet something told us that this wasn't the way of Bellhart. Bellhart posthumously saved his killer's life by carefully modeling professionalism and compassion for his Pennsylvania platoon.

In our weekly hospital staff meeting later, our commander called our efforts "Geneva Convention 101." He recalled our annual training video that teaches us to treat enemy combatants in the same way we treat our own wounded – even to the point that we must protect them from our own staff who might wish them harm.

Our enemy combatant stayed for six more weeks of both inpatient and impatient treatment. He visited our OR four more times where surgeons, inspired by the tourniquet story, worked to save the leg. In the end, they amputated his leg, but few of us felt satisfaction. We knew that Iraq had no wheelchair ramps and no laws to protect amputees. The insurgent would be permanently disfigured and forever shunned by his society.

Eventually, we discharged our patient to three bearded American men in civilian clothes and sunglasses. They flashed credentials and mumbled something about National Security. We never saw the insurgent again, but our staff remained content that we had done the right thing – the Bellhart thing. Despite ourselves, we topped impossible odds and we loved our enemy.

CHAPTER 9

VENGEANCE ISN'T CHEAP

As March came to an end, star-shouldered generals gathered for morning meetings to plan troop transfers from Iraq into Afghanistan. None of them seemed to require our input, so Peoples and I spent our time talking about the slight increase in temperatures. I suppose it was our way to coax the rain to end and the summer to begin because hot days meant that our tour was over. I'd anticipated the warmer weather by switching my wake-up drink from hot chocolate to the frozen chai lattes sold in our Green Beans Coffee shop. Like the theater, Green Beans helped us believe we weren't really at war. Who's going to kill a guy with a cappuccino in his hand?

During one of those morning discussions, Peoples excused himself to go the bathroom. He returned with some intel. "We got a big trauma coming in."

"How do you know that?"

He pointed to the ceiling speakers. "Wait for it. Wait for it."

"Trauma call. Trauma call. Trauma times four," the unseen voice said.

How does he do that? I didn't have time to ask, but I did suggest he fix his unbuttoned fly.

"It's about 15 minutes out," he said.

"What else do we know?" I reached for my notebook and fed the trashcan a half-consumed chai.

"Nothin' really. They're just saying it's bad: three Americans and their Iraqi translator.

"Just pray they aren't part of the 3 percent," I mumbled.

Peoples took a minute to do the math, not something he did well unless it was to measure shelves for the chapel supply cabinet he was building.

"Right," he said. Peoples could be slow, but we both knew that Balad's mortality rate was 3 percent. Of course that meant we saved 97 percent. In fact, platoon and squad leaders often promised wounded soldiers that if they could get their "sorry ass" to our hospital they would have a 97.4 percent chance of seeing their friends and family again. What they probably didn't calculate were the odds of actually *seeing* their friends again, because sometimes soldiers lost their eyes. No one quoted the statistics of soldiers actually able to embrace their families, because sometimes soldiers lost arms. And no one calculated the unspeakable possibility that they'd not make love to their spouses again, because well, sometimes soldiers lost that too.

"Maybe we can hedge their odds." I nodded toward our newly built supply shelves and Peoples took the hint by grabbing a few Bibles along with a fistful of rosaries. Beyond knowing ETAs, we knew little of what religious support we needed for the incoming wounded, so we often snatched whatever we could pack in our ABU cargo pockets. In my rush to exit the office, I nearly plowed into Peoples who had abruptly stopped in the doorway.

"Just a sec," he said. "I'm gonna call our priest and let him know he might be needed." His wisdom made me wonder, *Who was this garbage collector?* Whoever he was, he was learning hospital ministry fast. When I heard him ask the priest to relay our request to the rabbi, I knew he had this wired.

A minute later, we stood in the ER nursing station eavesdropping on the radio chatter between our hospital and the incoming helicopter. The onboard flight nurse said they were "incoming with one ambulatory and four expectants." He revised their ETA by five minutes because they had "flat BPs and a CPR in progress." The ruddy young radioman promised the flight nurse that we'd be ready, even though he likely felt what we were all feeling – there was no way to be ready for this.

Five minutes later, we heard the swop-swop-swop of the twin-bladed Blackhawk UH-60L on final approach into the February sun. The helo kicked gravel bits on the backside of our emergency room, signaling specially trained stretcher-bearers to go to the helo pad with two-wheeled contraptions that resembled a cot. The stretchers were affixed to a rickshaw and balanced by bicycle wheels that allowed for a quick pivot in tight spaces.

Within moments, a parade of eight medics pushed four gurneys through the swinging doors like they were running to a firefight. Determined staff docked each gurney into curtained cubicles while teams of experts stood with gloved hands held at shoulder height waiting for orders. Steely doctors expelled Hail Mary orders in a prayer for the impossible.

Trauma responses are timed and the seconds are filled with the intensity of a final quarter in a close-scoring basketball game. If we couldn't clear patients from the ER within 30 minutes, game over. Precious seconds ticked by in a room immersed in absolute anarchy. I was leaning so far over the line, hoping the staff would call for their chaplain, that I was half expecting someone to call me on a line foul.

That's about the time I locked eyes with a young lieutenant walking toward me and cradling his flight helmet with the cocky confidence of a Top Gun. He had a shaved head and bloody nose, but he carried the unyielding bent of a military academy graduate. My first guess was that his Ray-Bans made him a flight nurse just as he likely figured my stiffened stance and gray hair made me a doctor. It didn't matter to him whether I was a doctor or chaplain; he was the one giving the orders.

"Take care of my guys first, Doc!" he said. His expression commanded me to understand what he meant.

I understood.

"Absolutely. We will, but I'm just the chaplain," I said.

If he heard that, he didn't much care. He simply raised a bloodied hand to display his second priority. "I think I took a bullet too," he said.

My first thought was *Oh God, they shot the flight nurse*, but before I had a chance to react, our chief nurse stepped from behind me.

"Let's take a look at that, son," said Colonel William Osprey. At six-foot-six, the nurse fit the stereotype of a high-ranking doctor or at least an aging linebacker. He cradled the lieutenant's hand and examined it at the distance required by his farsighted eyes.

"We'll be taking care of that now, son," he said. He motioned his nursing team to sequester the lieutenant in the urgent care room adjoining the ER. I followed the team into the curtained cubicle where the staff peppered the 26-year-old platoon leader with pre-surgical questions designed to distract him.

"What's your name? What unit are you from? When did this happen?" I've heard the same rapid-fire questions from ER clerks at home when they interview the parent of a critically injured pediatric patient. While the answers are sometimes helpful, the questions stall the inventible telling of bad news.

The lieutenant didn't want any bad news, but he spoke in staccato sentences like a POW releasing guarded information to interrogators. He wasn't the flight nurse at all. He was Jim Young, serial number 555-12-1234, and for the past 15 months he'd commanded the 5th Squadron from the 1st Cavalry Regiment, 1st Stryker Brigade Combat Team, 25th Infantry Division out of Fort Wainwright, Alaska.

"Please make sure they are taking care of my guys," he said. He didn't have to say it twice. I stepped outside the curtain and into the main trauma room where I saw staff cutting off clothes and doctors barking orders for IVs and crash carts. I knew we were taking care of them when I saw Dr. Deavers circling his entourage around the patient in Trauma Bay No.1, Corporal Michael Muthart. The blond, blue-eyed, soldier was a 21-year-old former Eagle Scout from upstate New York, who everyone was hoping to include in the 97 percent of survivors. Nurses optimistically wheeled in the crash cart and pulled premeasured doses of epinephrine while technicians prepped blood test vials.

But Deavers didn't need to test for dead. He grabbed the defibrillator paddles, rubbed them together, and blended his orders with confidence and chance.

"Charge – clear – shock – charge – clear – shock."

Nothing.

"One ampule epinephrine." Deavers spoke with the demeanor of someone ordering a double espresso.

More compressions and more shock.

Heads turned to the monitor. Nothing.

Deavers placed his stethoscope on Muthart's chest.

"I'm calling it," he said.

"Anyone have any objections?"

I did, but said nothing. We'd been checkmated and Muthart joined the 3 percent club.

Deavers snapped loose his rubber gloves and exchanged them for fresh ones.

"Chap!" he called.

I joined Deavers at the gurney.

"We've pronounced. Can you say a few words?"

I looked down at the bare-chested soldier and placed my hand on his still warm forehead. *Say what?* I wondered. *What the hell kind of response did I have for what I saw in Muthart's open-eyed stare?* I wasn't ready for this. We saw the previous deaths coming from afar, down a long track. The warning signs began when the doctors labeled the soldiers "expectant." It signaled me that I'd be at bat in the upcoming hours while the staff withdrew life support. "Expectant" meant death would not surprise us.

But when I looked at Muthart's bullet-ridden body, I could see that it was a train wreck. It's as if Deavers had told me, "Bam! This dude is dead. Now say something profound, Chaplain, or just say something pretend. Say anything you want, but I gotta do something that'll really work."

I prayed a quick prayer, but Deavers wasn't waiting for a second opinion. He consigned Muthart to the three-percent report and crossed the room to supervise the team working on 21-year-old Corporal Daryl Norton of Minneapolis. The corporal hadn't gone down easy. According to the bits and pieces I had heard the lieutenant say earlier, "Norton was hit in the arm, went down, got his weapon, returned fire, took a round in the leg, went down, stood up, returned fire again, and took a shot to the chest."

Dr. Tamara Chin led the team working on Norton. The rusty-haired oncologist who did double duty in our ER stubbornly tried to reciprocate the corporal's determination. Chin called "clear" and then leaned on the paddles with all her 112 pounds to send nearly 1,000 volts through Norton's body in hopes of coaxing him back. Her grit made it seem as if she was listening to the voices of Norton's family urging her to work harder.

Perhaps she heard the rally of Norton's high school ROTC cadets say, "Give him epinephrine!" Possibly she gave the second and third shock on behalf of the grandfather who raised Norton. Whatever Chin heard or imagined, the staff seemed to work with an awareness of an unseen presence. Possibly they heard the pleading voice of Norton's fiancé, his elementary school sweetheart, who was planning a summer wedding. "Doctor, please, can't you try just one more time?"

One more shock. Once more, nothing.

"He's done, too," Deavers concluded. Chin nodded and her team agreed.

"Chap! Over here," Deavers called. I was standing right beside him, but he didn't see me because his hyper-focus compromised his peripheral vision

I took my position near Norton's head and got my first look at the kid. Like so many of them, he'd shaved his head for battle. His face and neck were smoothly tanned with desert experience. His ears settled in an off-center place where they seemed permanently vigilant for the danger he never heard coming.

I came to Iraq wanting to be close when soldiers died, and I was getting closer than I imagined. Norton shared the same age and rank as my Marine son, Michael. His arm tattoos matched the ones my son wore. This was as close as I dared get, no closer. But before I could measure the words to pray, I heard a third request.

"Chap! Over here!" called the Czar.

I raised my dazed expression from Norton's gurney and stumbled over to Specialist Michael Almond, where I saw another endgame.

Almond had the shaven face of an ashen 31-year-old experienced fifth grade teacher from Stevens Elementary School. Almond often told his squad about leaving his teaching job, two kids and a wife in Stevens County, Utah, so he could "fight for his country."

"Can you say another prayer?" asked a face in the crowd.

If she meant, "Did I have another prayer," the answer was no. None of the other prayers worked. They were all dead. I couldn't do resurrectory prayers, but I prayed anyway.

When Almond joined the 3 percent, silence briefly enveloped our room like a dust storm. All I could hear was the simultaneous snapping sound made by staff removing their elastic gloves in disgust as we realized that the three soldiers were dead on arrival. The interpreter had taken two headshots and was already in the morgue.

"We're done here, people," said Deavers. "Nothing more to see."

With that, I walked back to the red line where Peoples was hanging up the phone in the nurse's station. He phoned in a play-by-play to our boss, Chaplain Hearts, who was sending for the priest and the rabbi. Peoples stepped from behind the counter, put a broad hand on my back, and tried to find the eyes I wouldn't give him. We all felt so useless: me with my ineffectual prayers, the staff with their last-ditch efforts, and the lieutenant in his inability to save his men. There was nothing anyone could do: no prayers to say, no drugs to administer, no resuscitations to be made. What had seemed like forty-five minutes of hard work took place in less than ten.

"Come on, let's help the PAT," Peoples suggested. The PAT was the Patient Administration Team who sifted through the personal effects of the dead. It was a job no one wanted, and those who worked to save lives usually kept their distance from the PAT. However, Peoples and I worked somewhere between the middle of helping the living and honoring the dead. So we busied ourselves pulling dog tags from their chests or from their boots. We stripped patches from their uniforms and went through pockets taking pens, coins, and papers. Beside me, a PAT airman removed pictures of Almond's wife standing with two small children.

"Are you alright?" I asked. She wiped her eyes on her shoulder and seemed young enough to be Almond's sister.

"Yes," she lied. Like me, the bleary-eyed airman had hoped to put the soldier on a breathing machine so we could medevac him to Germany. Once there, a chaplain could say a prayer, doctors would withdraw life support, and his family could watch the heart-monitor line go flat.

When we were done, I walked back to the exam room where the "L-Tee" sat shaking his head and twitching nervously at the news confirming the death of his team members. Lt. Young explained how his squad had been searching a house when they uncovered a "spider hole" much like the one where the disheveled Saddam Hussein hid. The squad surrounded the hole and pointed their muzzles, affixed with flashlights, down the tunnel. Like the jack-in-the-box in the childhood toy, an insurgent popped out and sprayed the room with fire. At least two of our DOAs died before they knew it. The two surviving members of the squad returned fire and killed the insurgent.

I couldn't help but recall how I'd used the same tactic during my boyhood war-games when I'd pop from a garbage can, brace a broom handle off my hip and sweep it across my flank, baptizing the approaching Landers brothers with a hail of imaginary lead. But this was no game. This wasn't play. Our soldiers weren't able to stand and sneak away like Dennis Landers did when I "shot" him in the garbage can ambush.

"We got the SOBs," the lieutenant said. "They were bad guys who tortured women and children. We paid a terrible price, but we got them." He spoke in language soldiers often hide from their chaplain, but I nodded in sympathetic agreement, both to his assessment and to his vengeful tone. A few minutes later, patient transport arrived to wheel the lieutenant into surgery.

I left Peoples in the ER to greet the arriving priest, retreated to my office, and shut the door, ostensibly to plan the Fallen Warrior Ceremony. I tried to work, but all I could say was, "Lord, God, oh God. Why?" I got nothing, so I withdrew into my childhood picture of war where I could see myself blasting the SOBs that did this.

Suddenly, I slammed my fists into my desk and amended my prayer with words no one, and I mean not even my wife or closest friend, has ever heard me say. No one, that is until Peoples pushed open the door and entered without warning.

"Chaplain, are you all right?" he said.

"I will be." It seemed as if lying should be more difficult.

Over the next few hours, but before end-of-shift, we conducted a triple Fallen Warrior Service. At the half-hour ceremony, I acknowledged the uselessness we all felt while trying to resuscitate dead men. When I spoke of my own desire for revenge, startled people looked up from their boots they'd recently bleached of blood.

"The Bible says 'Vengeance is mine, says the Lord,'" I quoted, "But most of us are feeling we'd like a piece of the murderous insurgents that killed our guys."

I wanted to shred my Geneva Convention claim as a non-combatant. According to the outdated rules, I wasn't allowed to kill or be killed. If captured, I was supposed to pray and conduct religious services for both sides. More pretend games. The insurgents hadn't read the rules. That day I wanted to kill for God. God couldn't have revenge because I wanted it. And I would get it–vicariously, at least.

Later that night, I shuffled into DFAC where the bulging crowd forced me to eat in an unfamiliar corner occupied by three F-16 pilots from south Florida. I exchanged pleasantries, and we quickly established common ground since I had been stationed in Florida where I had once helped recover the body of one of their pilots.

The squadron leader, a tall balding man about my size, told me his squadron spent the last fifty-eight days of their sixty-day rotation doing almost nothing – until that day. In non-specific detail, he said they'd dropped their bombs on some really "bad guys."

I yawned and offered my day's story with a top-this tone. The pilots returned a look of familiarity.

"Chaplain," the squadron leader said. "We know the incident you're talking about. After your patients were medevac'd from that house, we bombed the crap out of the place."

"Oh, sorry, Chaplain," he said. It was rehearsed embarrassment, but he continued. "Honest to God, there was nothing left."

For the first time, I sat straight in my chair. "You got the bastards," I said.

They glared at me like I had just revealed classified information. I suppose I had. Nevertheless, I imagined myself in their cockpit knowing what I now knew, aiming the cannon for a tight and personal shot. I would, and pardon my chaplain cliché, blow them to hell.

"Fellas, you just made my day," I told them. And I meant it. For it seemed on that day that vengeance didn't belong to God or me. I felt unashamedly grateful that vengeance found a surrogate in the cockpits of four screaming F-16s.

CHAPTER 10

WASTING AWAY IN MORTAR-RITA-VILLE

I slapped my vibrating cellphone to cancel the alarm and then pushed my fingertips deep into my eye socket. I was trying to extract the reason I'd set my alarm for 0530 on Easter Sunday. Finally I remembered how I'd promised to help my colleagues in the base chaplain's office to make sound checks for our open-air Easter worship service. We punned the event as the "Son-Rise Service," and scheduled it for 0700 in a soccer stadium that Saddam had built.

I sat up to stretch and pushed my fists into my lower back until I heard the chiropractic pop of relief. I'd slept fitfully under the early morning gunfire of something called a C-RAM, Counter Rocket, Artillery, and Mortar. The gun was a US Navy transplant normally used at sea to fell anti-ship missiles, but was retrofitted for land use. It stood about a thousand yards from my hooch where it worked like a giant Gatling gun, automatically firing a defensive umbrella of lead against the Vietnam-era mortars insurgents lobbed over our 30-foot fences.

The guns sounded very much like the fluttering tongue sound I used as a child to simulate the rattle of a machine gun. Those were the days I'd use my well-practiced aim to "shoot down" enemy planes from the darkening San Francisco sky or ambush unwary patrols of eight-year-olds as they tried flanking our perimeter through the tall summer grass.

The C-RAM was noisier of course, but it wasn't the noise that kept me awake. What kept me awake was the simple realization that someone wanted to kill me, and after me, kill someone else. But most assuredly, and most personally, they wanted me dead. While there were some chaplains who saw Balad as their "Chaplain Rambo ministry," the C-RAM humbled most of us to parody a Jimmy Buffet song into "Wasting Away in Mortar-rita-ville."

I slipped out of my bunk and into the uniform I had draped on my bedside chair. I took a deep breath to button my pants and shuffled into my shirt before accessorizing with a soft hat and muddy boots. I pushed open my hooch's spring-loaded door and stepped into the hazy morning where I immediately saw why the guns had been so active. A sandy curtain encased the base, providing the ideal cover conditions for insurgents to launch their mortars. I walked along an open trail and was halfway to the stadium when the C-RAM's renewed flutter reminded me of a dining conversation I'd had with a Navy corporal midweek.

The sailor and two of his shipmates randomly took picnic-table seats across from me in the dining hall during a crowded Wednesday evening of steak and lobster. Two of the men were smaller and took subservient seats on each side of the corporal, a supersized sailor with a sloping midsection that said he'd grown fond of land-based dining. Our meeting was made even more rare by the fact that our base had more chaplains than the navy had total personnel on base. The oversized sailor was making room for his two over-loaded plates when he noticed my cross.

"Hey, Chaps! How you doing?" he asked. He offered the wide grin of a naval greeting.

"Good! Even better in 30 days!" I said.

"Two weeks for me." He was the kind of guy who put two syllables in every "damn," and we quickly became 30-minute best friends. We swapped stories of our deployment, mine at the hospital and his on the firing end of a C-RAM.

"Thanks for what you guys do," I said. "It helps me sleep."

The gunner snickered at his silent shipmates, hinting at an undisclosed discrepancy.

"What's funny?" I asked.

"Sounds like someone believes the junk briefed in newcomer's orientation," he told his shipmates. Both gave the big man the polite smile of an audience member.

My new friend leaned over a line of condiments and offered his best stage whisper. "Truthfully, Chaps, of all the times our C-RAM engaged incoming targets I can't remember a single, successful intercept."

"What the...?" I stopped myself. The newcomer's briefer claimed that the C-RAM shot down 65 percent of the incoming mortars.

"Yeah, well, uh.... Here, let me demonstrate," he offered. He slid a peppershaker to his edge of the table and then checked his six for incoming superior officers.

"The problem is that the insurgents launch their shells on a shallow trajectory."

"Swoosh," he said before lifting the shaker into an arc toward my end of the table. "The damn thing comes in too low for our warning system to detect. Then, boom!" The mock explosion peppered my briny plate.

"Nice," I said.

"They just shoot and scoot," he whispered.

I pushed my plate aside. "I think it's time for me to 'scoot' over and get some ice cream now," I said. I stood to leave, but he revised his volume to project over scraping plates and moving chairs.

"Don't worry. Most of the rockets are old duds."

A stream of laughter erupted on my exit, but I did hear one seaman warn the group that it was "bad luck to scare the Chaps."

The recollection quickened my steps toward the coliseum. I couldn't help but think how my navy friends were defending our ground with an attitude of *Que sera* while the insurgents boldly fired mortars from exposed ground using the equivalent Muslim attitude of *Insha'Allah,* or God willing.

I arrived an hour before start time to find a stadium smaller than our stateside coliseums, but replete with concrete decor. The booths, the benches, the inside walls seemed to float like giant colorless icebergs in a sea of frozen concrete. The gray dreariness gave an eerie reminder of the malevolence we were hoping to vanquish.

According to Balad lore, Iraqi athletes once came to the stadium where they were forced to kick a concrete soccer ball. It became a really bad day when the coach turned out to be Uday Hussein, Saddam's brother and head of the National Iraqi Olympic Committee. He forced some athletes to crawl on newly poured asphalt while he beat them and threw some players from a bridge. Several losing members of the 1994 Iraqi World Cup soccer team were apparently unmotivated by that practice, so Uday mercifully shot them.

On the hastily constructed wooden stage, I untangled a pile of microphone cords and had barely finished connecting them at 0659 hours when a ruddy second lieutenant took the podium. He pulled the microphone down to his height and the resulting squawk sent me scrambling for an anonymous seat. The lieutenant shot nervous glances to the nearby perimeter fence and then began his customary safety briefing in a liturgical drone.

"In the event the base takes mortar fire," he told the congregants, "assume the prone position with your eyes and ears covered. Wait for one minute before running for shelter." He concluded the briefing with all the feigned annoyance of an Irish flight attendant expecting a "wee-bit" of turbulence. "Hopefully our C-RAM will answer any trouble."

"Amen, but fat chance," I mumbled.

"Bad Chaplain," I added. My pew mate's glance told me that my unconscious self-scolding was an audible comment. I should be more respectful. After all, the lieutenant had a thankless task given him by some officer who obviously had no desire to see the Son rise. My unchecked cynicism exposed the pretense of my presence. I had told Peoples that I was going to the service to help with podium arrangements, but the truth was that I had come to find something or, more likely, to just get away from something. I wasn't sure.

Sara, my arm-waving nurse, followed the lieutenant to the podium to lead the congregational singing. Within a few minutes, I felt myself being pulled into a robust chorus usually reserved for marching soldiers chanting an off-color jody. I don't know why, but men often sing deeper and tougher when they are deployed. Perhaps they sing a subconscious serenade to their absent loved ones, or maybe theirs is a melodic prayer to mute their fear. I am not sure. Our melody resounded off the dew-dampened gray of the bunkered concrete, and I prayed for the enemy to hear us. I wanted our harmony to be his siren for change. I wanted to convince him that we could all change our tune from war to peace. I knew I was being desperately naïve. Most likely he heard our music the same way I perceived the music spewing from the minarets – a wiry and tangled disharmony. He probably heard our music as psychological warfare – I could only hope that our worship would change us, transport us, resurrect our fading spirit, if only until breakfast.

I withdrew my attention from the desert stretches and found that Chaplain Terry Wilson of the Kansas National Guard had already begun his sermon. Wilson was a wiry guy with an unpretentious smile who made endless shaping gestures from opposing hands. He preached about the crucifixion of Jesus with a personal conviction like he had been nailed to a few crosses himself. He quarried his words from an authentic place as he read the last words of Jesus, "Father, forgive them for they know not what they do."

"Easter became the first real suggestion among world religions of anything like a resurrection," he said. "Jesus showed us that death was a momentary thought, a slight detour and then, you get up and walk!"

Just like my childhood friends playing war? Maybe it was a do-over in "a better place." Anywhere would have to be better than here.

Suddenly, an Easter chorus of pagers interrupted Wilson's sermon, sounding much like the back-up signals of two-dozen trucks. Wilson paused as an electronic leash jerked medical personnel from their stony bleachers and out the exits toward the hospital. Apparently the enemy hadn't seen our Son-Rise PowerPoint proclaiming Easter to be a down-day. *Please, no death today,* I prayed with sardonic silence, *at least not until we finish our Easter ham. Bad Chaplain.*

A few minutes later, I flashed my ID to the hospital gate guard while a Black Hawk UH-60L helo docked in an all-too familiar heliport. I made my way through the hospital halls and into the ER where a full trauma team attended our first patient, Specialist First Class Victoria Martin.

Trauma Bed No.1 was the closest to my red line and I could see that Victoria was a dark-haired woman who looked like she was still having trouble finding five-foot-two. When I looked below her acned face, I saw rippling arm muscles that suggested as much strength in her body as she showed in her character. Technicians cut away her burned uniform while our doting ophthalmologist worked to remove shrapnel from her forehead and right eye.

Victoria also had a complex fracture in her left hand, but she seemed as if she was going to be mostly okay.

For the briefest of moments, I rewound my mind to the worship service where I'd been 15 minutes earlier. We were preaching hope, singing love, praying peace, and now we were at war again. It was as if no one had heard our music or our prayers. The venue change was tough to process because it felt like we were fickle kids switching between games at the whim of the group bully.

I rematerialized when I overheard Victoria talking to everyone, but no one in particular.

"I couldn't save him! He's dead isn't he?"

"Who?" someone asked.

"Sgt. Magdaleno," she said. "I should have saved him. I'm a medic."

The attending nurse injected Martin with pain medication and added her soothing assurance. "It's okay. You're safe now."

When the medication took hold, Martin described the incident for which she would later receive an Army Commendation Medal, complete with a "V" for Valor. She was a ride-along guest on a mission outside Karbala when their vehicle hit an EFP, an Explosively Formed Projectile. The EFP did what it was designed to do and sent molten steel tearing through their armored vehicle. In the moments following the blast, the half-blinded Martin grabbed her medical kit and felt her way through the twisted hot rubble to find her team leader, SGT Raul Magdaleno.

What she couldn't find was Magdaleno's left leg. It had been amputated just below the hip by the explosion. Barehanded and half-blind, the young medic reached past a twisted pelvic anatomy and into a tangled weave of muscle, bone, and ligaments until she reached her destination – the femoral artery. Warm life drenched her hand by the time she finally pinched the artery closed and began counting his pulse. Each beat felt in her fingers was a countdown to death.

"You did the right thing," our trauma czar assured her. "That's what we would have done."

"But I couldn't maintain my hold," she said.

"That's because it was impossible," countered the Czar. "There is no way to maintain that effort, even in our Operating Room." Everyone worked to assure Martin that in the moments in which she had held the artery closed; she was literally the Dutch Boy with his finger in the dike.

"He has a daughter named Priscilla and a baby on the way."

No one had an answer for that one, so she added more details.

"He told me how much he loved his wife, Tina, and didn't want to leave her. He hated this damn war."

Sara, the surgical nurse, stepped up to ask her when she had last eaten.

"Not since breakfast at zero-six," she said.

"Just relax, now. You're safe." The nurse kept saying it until Martin was in the safety of sleep.

As Martin mercifully slipped into unconsciousness, I made my way to the other side of the room where Private First Class Raymond Costa lay wounded from shrapnel to his left leg and a head concussion. The PFC was an African American whose set jaw and soft brown eyes told me he wanted to tell his story.

"Hi, Private," I said. My tone shifted to the one I had often used with my fevered teen. "I'm Chaplain Burkes."

Costa didn't say anything at first and I wondered if he might be the kind of patient who assumes the chaplain comes in the role of the Grim Reaper.

"You don't have to talk," I said. "I'm not here to convert you, convince you, or even baptize you. I'm just here. Would you like to..."

"We shouldn't have been on that road." His words rolled over mine, so I stood still and waited for more.

"Martin tried to help our sergeant, but she was so badly hurt that another squad had to drag her out. I don't think Magdaleno made it." His conclusion felt concussive.

"All I know is that the three of you are here in our hospital," I said. "Maybe Magdaleno is somewhere else." He was, of course, "somewhere else" – the refrigerated trailor outside the emergency room known as "the refer." I gave an elusive response partly because I wasn't authorized to tell him anything, but mostly because I was still fighting my own fear that he would ask me to explain how God let this happen. But he didn't ask that. Actually, he upped the verbal ante when he said, "What's the purpose in all of this?"

Nearby, Costa's battle buddy strained to hear our conversation. Specialist Anthony Thomas was a balding half Italian who looked old enough to have avoided the hazards of war. He had a back injury but was still able to turn his head to hear my answer.

I took a deep breath and sunk my chin into my chest, a self-conscious effort to appear thoughtful. I didn't feel like giving him the "hearts and minds" speech or advocating the "liberation of Iraq." Besides, I wasn't sure if I believed any of that myself anymore.

He persisted with the questions. "Why are we doing this? These people don't want us here."

I checked my spiritual pockets, much like my father had done, absentmindedly patting his suit while searching for his wallet or small New Testament. My pockets felt empty and I flushed at the thought that Costa had caught me without an answer book. I exhaled relief when I heard the saving voice of our bespectacled radiologist.

"Sorry, Chaplain," he said. "We have to get our patients to MRI."

Our trauma treatment was designed for speed, and we took less than 20 minutes to triage the squad into varying tests or surgeries. Those of us who were nonessential to the process sat in our offices or behind nursing stations gobbling boxes of Easter Marshmallow Peeps sent by the Military Mothers at Home. I ate a few Jesus Peeps and then returned to the hospital chapel. I still had to conduct my weekly 1100 worship service where I found Peoples pacing the pews.

"Where you been?" he asked. Somehow he hadn't heard the trauma call and was surprised to see me a bit disheveled.

"Talk later," I said before I began greeting the first arrivals.

Twenty-six people squeezed into our little chapel that morning, some still wearing their bloodied boots. Halfway through my sermon, Staff Sgt. Peoples slipped across the hall to answer our office phone. He returned a few minutes later making a winding motion with his hands like a movie director. The man had gall; I'd give him that. I followed his cue and shortened the sermon. When I finished, I made my way to the backdoor and shook a few shaky hands.

Peoples disappeared again and just as I wondering how I'd reprimand him for the interruption, he reappeared telling me PFC Costa wanted to see me. I nodded to the remaining few parishioners who'd heard Peoples' request and knew they understood my need for a quick exit. I took a shortcut through a hallway office and entered through the backdoor of the Intermediate Care Unit.

I found Costa in stall No. 7 where he'd pulled his surrounding bed curtain closed.

"Knock-knock," I said from outside his cubicle.

The pause felt deafening.

"Knock-knock," I repeated. "It's the chaplain."

"Come in," he said. I slid the curtain across the ceiling tracks and saw him staring at the wall opposite my entry side.

"Hey, Private."

He answered with a slow rotation toward me. Bloody scratches reddened his dark complexion and when he opened his eyes he asked, "Are you the chaplain?" He answered his own question before I could remind him of our earlier meeting.

"Could you bring me a Bible?" he asked. It was a request I heard as testing my ecclesiastical legitimacy.

"Sure," I said.

"I lost mine in the blast."

"Sure, I will bring you a Bible," I said. "No problem."

I stood hushed for a moment, not knowing what else to say. I felt somehow that I had intruded into a conversation he was having in another dimension and interrupted his colloquy with an unseen guest. Whether the guest was God himself or the disembodied Magdaleno, or both, he didn't or couldn't say.

"Anything else I can do?" I asked.

I needed that to be all he needed, but of course there was more. Costa had seen his friend die on Easter in the same manner Jesus died – from exsanguination, colloquially known as "bleeding out." In the quiet following the explosion, he'd even heard Sergeant Magdaleno say, "My wife wants a girl."

Yes, there was something else Costa needed. He leaned toward me like a relay runner stretching to relinquish the baton and said, "I want you to pray, Chaplain." The lilt in his voice implied an incomplete sentence. It was as if he wanted to say, "I've been praying ever since I was hit, and now I'm tired. It's your turn."

"What is that you would like me to pray?" I asked.

My question was a well-practiced one that I often asked in my civilian hospital. The problem was that eavesdropping family members or staff often saw my question as misunderstanding the obvious and assumed the patient to be clearly requesting a healing prayer. But it's not as clear as one might think. Not everyone wants to be healed. Nevertheless, Costa understood the question better than most. He'd seen the vapor of life dismissed by unseen malice. He shed his selfish concerns in search of a prayer much bigger than his own healing – a prayer that could stitch his world back together.

At first he answered with a question about the insurgents. "Don't they know we are trying to help them?"

I told him that I didn't think the insurgents saw our intervention as helpful. He looked away and appeared to be disappointed with that possibility. Then he interrupted the stillness with his request.

"Chaplain, could you pray that the people who did this will soon understand that we are here to help them and make their country better?"

I felt my neck stiffen, but I managed to promise him that I would do that. "After all," I said, "the Bible does say 'Pray for your enemies.'"

His eyebrows furrowed a bit before he responded. "Yes, but it says more than that. It says we have to forgive. I need you to pray that God will forgive the insurgents that did this."

My voice faltered, and I unconsciously shook my head from side to side. "I'm sorry. Pray that…?" For a moment I stood wondering what my expressions were telling him. I reminded myself to stay focused, exude conviction, and radiate certainty, but I had no real answer for Costa outside the range of habitual chaplain answers. I was lost in space, lost in the clinical space where I had presumed myself to be an accomplished navigator, lost where I thought I once knew faith.

I tried to hold my professional ground by posing a clinical question. "What would that prayer sound like?" His request was clear, but my question sounded like I was fumbling with a forgotten password. Maybe I was.

"Use that prayer Jesus prayed," he said. "You know, the one he prayed on the cross."

I paused, trapped in the simplicity of the request. Then, like a muscled-man pulling hand-over-hand on my rescue rope, his request dragged my faith out of the hole where it was trapped.

"You know the prayer," he said. "'Father, forgive them, for they know not what they do.'"

Of course I knew it. It was the prayer that Chaplain Wilson preached that morning when we got the trauma call. Jesus prayed it as he, too, bled out, but he wasn't praying for himself; he prayed for the mob that unjustly crucified him. Jesus saw his killers not as evil, but as ignorant – ignorant of the complicity they assumed in their own downfall. In fact, I'd heard many sermons make the point that Jesus' prayer not only sought forgiveness for his tormenters, but forgiveness on behalf of succeeding generations – a prayer for me, for Costa, and for the insurgents.

In wartime hospitals, it is heroically common for soldiers with missing limbs or other ghastly wounds to beg the doctors to take care of their buddies first. They commonly ask the chaplain to pray not for them, but for their battle buddies. But Costa's prayer request to forgive the insurgents sent me into near-uncharted spiritual territory.

"I think that's a great prayer, Private." I said. Still I felt confused. Was I placating his battlefield shock or my naiveté? Or neither? Nevertheless, I bowed my head, shut my eyes and prayed aloud.

"God, Costa wants you to forgive the people that did this to his squad. He wants you to love them like you love him. This isn't going to make sense to most people, God, but I guess love rarely does make sense. Forgive these insurgents, for as you said on the cross, 'they know not what they do.' Amen."

Then, in the moment after my "amen" and before I opened my eyes, I saw a mental storyboard, a bloodied collage, a sort of silhouetted reenactment. I saw the insurgents planting their bomb, the detonation, Martin struggling to take care of her squad, Magdaleno bleeding out, and Costa praying for them all.

Suddenly that image blurred into two images, two worlds, two interpretations. One world was an unending circle of revenge, a twisted sphere of bloodied sinew, a place where reprisal and payback are exacted by legions of soldiers against unseen terrorists. The second world, seen only through the faith of this perceptively sagacious soldier, hinted at what the 9-11 aftermath could have been if forgiveness had been proclaimed instead of vengeance.

⅄ ⅄ ⅄

The next morning, I met with the nightshift chaplain, Rachel Davis, for our daily change-of-shift debriefing. Davis, a shorthaired African American woman, had perfected the poker face. She hid her thoughts behind narrow eyes and tucked them into near wordless conversations. I met her in our shared office each morning where she gave her monotone recital of patient-charting notes without ever looking at me or soliciting my counsel. On Costa's first night in the hospital, Davis read her report as usual, but when she got to Costa's name, she stared straight ahead into my chest and then tilted her head to meet my eyes.

"I guess you met Costa," she said.

"Sure did. Did he ask you to…."?

She wasn't yet taking questions, so she pushed ahead with a deep breath. "The guy is full of meds and couldn't sleep, so he called me to request a midnight prayer."

"What did he ask you to pray?"

Davis tugged at the embroidered cross insignia above her left breast pocket. "He asked me to pray that God would forgive the insurgents that killed his team leader."

"Same here," I said.

For a few minutes Davis and I looked at the mud-streaked floor and complained about how Peoples never swept the place. Then she abruptly said goodbye and went back to her hooch.

In the following few days Costa enlisted several other chaplains to pray for his enemy. After each chaplain prayed, he or she returned to the base chapel with the same expressions of incredulity. On the third day after Easter, Costa and his crew were medevac'd to Germany, so I can't say what happened to him after that. My guess is that he prayed that same prayer a few hundred times more. I even suspect that it's a prayer he is still praying today – a prayer that will be answered, if not in this world, then possibly in the next.

Four months later, Mrs. Tina Magdaleno delivered the baby girl she was praying for. She named her baby Mia, just as Sergeant Raul Magdaleno had requested.

CHAPTER 11

WHAT ARE YOU PRAYING FOR?

A few weeks later, it was my turn to see the doctor. It was time for my out-processing physical. It was time for me to go home.

But as I was getting ready to go to my appointment, I heard the piercing overhead speakers declare the arrival of a single trauma patient. Peoples and I took a brisk walk down a short L-shaped hallway from my office and pushed through the swinging doors of the Emergency Department to find Army Sergeant Robert Stevens of Clarksville, Ky. As were most of these calls, the staff was pretty busy and the patient was not ready for an extended chaplain visit, but I was able to introduce myself and promise a future visit.

The next day I found the sergeant recovering in our medium care unit.

Stevens was a member of the 194th Military Police Company from Fort Campbell who was leading a truck convoy from Fallujah. He'd held a finger at the corner of his eye to show me the peripheral side on which he'd first seen a teenager throwing an object off a balcony. As the object came into view, Stevens noticed it was making a long intentional arch and had deployed a ragged parachute.

His description reminded me of the parachutes I made while playing soldier as a kid. Everything I knew about parachutes, I'd learned from the 60s television show called Ripcord. The show produced a $1.98 toy plastic parachute made with the consistency of a cheap sandwich bag. The toy included a heavy plastic army man you would attach with cheap kite string. When you tucked the chute into the opening on his back and threw him into the air, he would come floating to earth. After a few days of playing with it, most of us usually lost it to a power line or tore the paper rivets from the parachute.

When I didn't have a plastic army man, I'd fashion a parachute from my mother's kitchen towels and kite strings. Sometimes I'd attach my lunch pail or a rock and toss the package from the balcony of our campus apartments. Occasionally my physics experiment hit the ground with a thud. But, through trial and error, I usually found the right ratio of weight and parachute surface and would take great delight in my engineering genius as I watched my parachute catch an updraft and float several yards from the drop point.

I'm sure Stevens' attacker had done the same thing as a child, perhaps attaching a bolt to a handkerchief. While neither he nor I know anything about the net downward force on the payload being the force of gravity minus the force of air resistance (*Fnet = (9.81 m/s^2 x* Mass,) the young man did know what would work and which size cloth to use.

He carefully hung from his parachute an armor-piercing grenade that resembled the old stick grenades of WWII and Vietnam fame. The parachute retarded the descent of the Russian-made, armor piercing, hand grenade just long enough to orient on to the target. Normally a grenade would be no match for the high-sided armored vehicle Stevens was driving. His steel-clad chariot was a Mine Resistant Ambush Protected vehicle, otherwise called the MRAP. MRAPs are built with an elevated cabin that surrounds up to 3/4 of its height with flat thick side armor, but soldiers love them for what is underneath. Their "V" shaped hulls deflect any explosive forces originating below the vehicle, thereby greatly lessening the injuries to the passengers. By the time I'd arrived in Iraq, Time Magazine was reporting that MRAPs had reduced fatalities by 90%.

But, as the hospital S2 (Intelligence Officer) would tell me later, the boy wasn't aiming for the underside of the MRAP nor any part of the four-inch side armor. Using the latest insurgent technique, he was aiming for the driver where the grenade's shaped charge would penetrate Stevens' window. Stevens says the blast was like a "welding arc in front of my eyes" as it shot molten metal between his legs. Stevens was the target and it was personal.

With a casted arm and right leg, Stevens told me, "All I could think about was we've been hit! I need to know about my crew. I started yelling for my driver to push through. I was praying the whole way for my gunner and my driver to be OK."

Twenty minutes later, he commanded the MRAP into his battalion aid station, 20 minutes by air from Balad. Only then, after Battalion Aid assured him that his crew suffered only superficial injuries, did Stevens turn his attention to his own spiritual aid and requested his Mormon Lay minister.

"I put my faith in the Lord," he told me. "I was just praying, 'Take care of my guys and help me with the pain.'" However, his injuries were serious enough for medics to transport him to our hospital. While helicopter rotors turned like a blender mixing sand and sweat, his minister administered a blessing just before takeoff.

Stevens described his injuries to me as being, "Comparatively minor compared to the potential of this attack," I asked him about what could have potentially happened.

He looked away. "Don't tell anyone you saw me crying," asked the 15-year veteran. "Let's just say," he answered, "that with this type of attack, our survival was a testament to God watching out for us."

As he worked for composure, Stevens explained his well-timed fortune and how his crew had traded their vulnerable Humvee for the MRAP two days before the attack. He reasoned that the Humvee, with its soft undercarriage, would have been low hanging fruit to the most junior rookie of all insurgents.

"By the grace of God, we were in the MRAP, and the molten steel passed *between* my legs." He glanced at his legs – both intact. "All I need is a few surgeries with plates and screws."

Still, I wondered, if the steel had taken a leg, would Stevens still be claiming God's presence? Maybe. Maybe, because I think Stevens saw God's presence not in his own survival, but in the survival of his friends. "I don't want to leave my guys," he said. "They're my family. I'm so grateful to have my crew saved."

I knew God was watching, but I'd already seen too many die. The theology in which I was raised would have to question why God would save a Mormon and not the Christian soldier. Like my mother's survival of the Tornado, I wondered if God was only on watch certain hours? Blind luck or God's watchful eye? Stevens' theological interpretation gave me a question for the S2. The insurgent was armed for a MRAP hunt; if Stevens had been in his Humvee, might the boy have passed on the Humvee?

Soon, the nursing staff came to the bedside and began pushing buttons and disconnecting wires. "You're going home, Sergeant," said the Chief of Medical Staff Erica Stanton, an oncologist wearing flowered scrubs. "Your flight's leaving for Germany in two hours. Then, in a few days" his nurse added, intoning a musical pun, "you'll take the last plane to Clarksville home."

As I patted Stevens' uninjured shoulder and wished him goodbye, he nodded to the nurse, and in a breaking voice he added, "These guys are the real heroes!"

It was now time for us both to go home.

CHAPTER 12

FINAL APPROACH

Two weeks later, I'm chasing the morning sun across the Atlantic. Most of us are awake to hear the pilot of our chartered DC 10 announce that we will be landing in Baltimore within the next 30 minutes. A fatigued cheer goes up among the 168 military service members with whom I've shared the last 18 hours hopscotching through the Mideast and Europe. At the moment, I'm one landing and one plane connection away from my Sacramento homecoming. It's Cinco de Mayo of 2009. Most of us have spent the past four months in a war zone and a good many of us have spent the last ten hours sleeping in any position we could find comfort. Later, the National Transportation and Safety Board (NTSB), whose report meticulously detailed the next forty minutes, would say that our pilot had only slept four hours before he'd taken the controls in Leipzig, Germany.

The plane trip really started five days before at Joint Air Base Balad in Iraq. There in the midst of the ancestral homeland of the father of my faith, I had served as the senior chaplain for the base hospital since New Year's Day. However, my corner of that world looked nothing like the Garden of Eden found in ancient Mesopotamia and Babylonia. In fact, during the last month, the rains had caused it to look more like Noah's Flood.

Just five days ago, I walked into my hooch to retrieve my duffle bags and say goodbye to my roommate, Lt Col Bill Carol. There was another dust storm approaching and we both knew that this kind of obscure evening often invited enemy mortar fire and grounded flights. So, when Carol asked me if I was ready to go, I simply zipped the last flap of my camouflaged backpack marked with the "Chaplain Burkes" nametag and mumbled something short of optimism. "Guess so." I said.

He then told me that he'd just volunteered to stay another month. "Wow," I chimed, "another month is another ten grand." He flashed a withering expression that sent his glasses further down his nose.

"The good news is," he said, "I'll get a private room." He'd recently discovered that his rank entitled him to privacy, so suddenly the past four months of rooming with me – "just a major," – was inequitable. If he didn't get his own room, he was planning to file a complaint. I had no response to that.

Carol was a good guy, but I was suddenly overtaken with the tragic irony of my job. I'd spent the previous day praying with two soldiers with combat amputation of all four limbs. Now my roommate, whose only job was to "snooper-vise" a dozen chaplains doing baptisms and Bar Mitzvahs, wanted his due deference for a room. In the last 120 days, I'd said prayers over the bodies of eight army soldiers – that didn't count the bodies that went home in pieces. I was done counting bodies. I didn't give a rat's toot about his space. I was catching the next flight out of this hole and I was trying hard not to show the colonel my *kiss-my-butt attitude.*

When he asked me the perfunctory question about whether I was glad to leave, I admitted that I was glad to go home, but not exactly happy to leave. As an Air National Guard member, I was going home "out of cycle," two months sooner than the active duty counterparts; I felt like I was deserting my hospital team.

After a few more words, Carol offered to drive me to the passenger terminal to meet my chalk, the group of people scheduled to fly with me. There I found a passenger building not much different from the dozens of little terminals I'd transited in my civilian jobs. There was a long desk with customer service agents bowing over their computers, looking up only to announce the boarding of our flight. In an airport designed to load bombs, bullets, and boxes, passengers seemed more of a bother to the teams working the flightline.

Our group collected our boarding passes and then moved outside to the flightline where we started something called palletization, the act of strapping everyone's gear onto a 9' x 7' pallet for loading by forklifts. We moved quickly because it's not the safest place in the world.

Only a month before, a newly arrived airman named Luis Gutiérrez was processing some equipment when he felt a sting on his chest. After several minutes, he casually walked out of the night and into the back door of our emergency room, a little blood on his shirtless chest. He was the only patient of the evening, and we all assumed he'd scratched himself. I thought about chatting him up with some laid-back, "Where-are-you-from?" fluff, but I decided to return to my office to finish my charting duties.

A few minutes later, after having been examined more thoroughly, Luis requested to see a chaplain. When I arrived, our patient told me the story of how he'd just stepped off the plane from Colorado when he felt a slight prick. It turns out that the prick was a stray bullet fired by some yahoo off base. Celebratory fire is what it's called. Isaac Newton just named it the Third Law of Physics. What goes up must come down. Luis was laughing scared as he traced the bullet path with his finger from just between his nipples, tunneling below his skin, and resting near his belly button. A month later, a four-star general pinned the Purple Heart on Luis' uniform and used the opportunity to convince the news cameras of the justness of our battle. I'm not sure anyone noted the significance of the date, but it was April Fool's Day.

With our equipment loaded, we were able to hot-load the plane, which means we boarded our camouflaged C130 transport on a back ramp with propeller wash hitting us like a big blow dryer. We jammed into a web seat that extended the length of the aircraft like one big park bench and stared at our mound of palletted gear. Two hours later, we landed at Al Udeid Air Base in Qatar where the time was 0200. Pronounced, Al-u-deed, military members call it simply, The Deed. It's the Grand Central Station for Coalition Forces in the Mideast, but it was a party base in comparison to where I'd been. Personnel geeks briefed us that we would be allowed two beers per day, unfiltered wireless internet, hot meals, and a bunk – amenities that have long been abbreviated as, two hots and a cot. After our briefing, we went slinking into the night, lugging our bags, on a half-mile walk in search of our dorm style tent.

At sunrise, the tent got busy with the noise of 25 transient soldiers rifling through their bags for toiletries. I woke with a morning headache that made anger easy to find and I sat up looking for a target. Our tent was a mess of discarded candy wrappers and water bottles, but it was the rat near the entrance that sent me off in search of the first sergeant in charge of the barracks. When I found him, I wanted desperately to take him to Balad and show him how we'd closed the eyes of the dead, draped them with a flag, and sent their effects back home to mother. *Then, I'd ask him, "If we could do all that, First Sergeant, I'm just wondering, why the hell can't your guys keep a tent free of rats."* Of course, I didn't say any of that. I remained in my professional role, but I knew he might have heard my unspoken expletives because his eyes seem to wander between my major rank and my chaplain cross. Perhaps he was weighing whether to salute me or sedate me, pray for me or placate me. He chose the latter when he recorded my tent number and promised a quick a response. Later, I wondered if my reaction was common to servicemembers reintegrating into the irritations of everyday life.

As I walked back to my tent, I felt my headache subsiding. Maybe the emotional venting helped, but the clean air also played a part. The Balad air was nasty because we burned everything we discarded: everyday trash, broken furniture, excess combat equipment, office equipment, and even biological remains. Researchers at Stony Brook University in New York would later conclude that exposure to the infamous Balad Burn Pit caused seven percent of us to return with signs of serious lung injuries – a figure well above the rate of troops serving stateside.

By then, I was feeling the need for caloric self-medication. Since coming to war, I'd been eating my frustrations. The morale-boosting menus of steak, shrimp, french fries, and ice cream had put nearly 15 pounds on me. I walked over to the chow hall and picked out several selections from the serving stations that lined each wall. It was May Day, and the arrival of my first 100-degree day justified another serving of pie a la mode.

After two days of eating and sleeping, I bummed a ride to the passenger terminal to board the D-10, nicknamed Freedom Bird. This plane was every bit a commercial jetliner and it was the first thing that had me anticipating the civilian life. As I walked the aisle, I did the thing chaplains do –a grip-and-grin thing, nodding respectfully at the pre-boarded high-ranking officers we called PowerPoint jockeys. They had their seats of choice. No middle seats for them. I managed a short row with a window and the extra pillows that went with it. Coincidently, a chaplain assistant from another base found the next row forward and, for the next day and a half, we took in the ambience of almost every overseas flight I've ever taken – long layovers, a surly attendant or two, stale air, bad food, old movies, and cramped seating.

⅄ ⅄ ⅄

Finally, a flight attendant interrupts my thoughts for the ritual of returning our seats and trays to the upright positions. As military members we police our area by filling bags of trash passed by the crew. The purser gushes the standard of how they are so proud to be the ones taking us home. They thank us for our sacrifices and for serving our country. They mean it to be a genuine benediction, but their sentiment sounds like the buh-bye dismissals you get after a Disneyland ride.

But my mind isn't tracking the instructions. I'm wiping the condensation from the plane window and straining to become the first one who'll spot dry land. My thoughts are scattered. I am thinking of the wedding my wife and I will help plan for our oldest daughter, Sara. At the same time, I am grieving that her younger sister, Brittney, wants to move from our California home across country with our grandchildren. I'm wondering how we can help our youngest daughter, Nicole, who has made no real progress in her life since getting her GED last year. Tangled amongst all my thoughts is Becky, my wife of 30 years. My feelings about her are a complicated weave of the holy and the horny. The holy surrounds me with a profound sense of shelter brought by 30 years of wrestling with the vow, "for better or worse." The horniness, well, that's not something chaplains are immune to, nor would I want to be. Today, it brings me into the company of soldiers who have known it for centuries when returning from war.

On our approach, we see the blue skies recently cleared by a passing thunderstorm. The flight attendants are strapped against a bulkhead talking about how little rest they will find on this stop. Baltimore area residents are subconsciously leaning forward. At 500 feet, the autopilot gives the pilot control and we are on approach for a normal landing. While gliding several feet over the "Runway 3-4," our plane drastically drops and bounces hard on its nose gear. It's the kind of hard hit you take when you miscalculate your step from a distance and hit sooner than you expect. Security footage later would show a large puff of smoke where our wheels hit. Eyewitnesses would swear they thought the plane was going to flip as they watched it drift, pitch, and roll to the far right of the center of the runway.

Inside, the plane is bending; nothing is right. It is as if I can feel the group psyche clawing at the runway screaming, "No! We want to be home! We won't die here!" We are in a zero G experience as our plane bounces like a kid's balsa glider trying to make a wheeled landing on grass. We hit two more times, porpoising, each hit harder than the last. More gasps as a flight-suited passenger barks, "Get a hold of it!" Plastic molding snaps from our ceiling and a few metal emergency oxygen apparatuses swing before us like a kid's piñata. Several seat mechanisms snap the chairs backward into laps behind them.

My entire Iraq experience is down to this. In the last four months, I'd felt the blood from a dying man's brain splash around my boots, I'd felt the weight of a detached arm in my hand, and I'd lain spread-eagle as enemy mortars shook the ground around me. But none of that gave me as much thought about dying as this moment.

Passengers on the left windows see the yellow centerline while those on my side shout about the wing drifting over the grass. It feels like we are about to veer off the runway and cartwheel into a fireball like the two recent crashes of the FedEx DC-11s. *Oh my God, this is where I'm going to die.* I think. *Here in Baltimore? Please,* willing my commands on the pilot. *Just shut the engines down and ease the plane onto the soft grassland where we might have a chance to jump.*

The pilot ignores my thoughts. The cabin's security door is jarred open and several of us witness his frantic attempt to throttle up and return into the clouds of a departing thunderstorm. Again, come my thoughts. *You jerk! Don't take us back up there.* One part of me wants to be higher, far away from the place I nearly died a few seconds ago. The other part of me wants to be lower and to get this over with. A second encounter with the runway feels like it'll be double jeopardy with death.

But it's too late to return to normal. The pilot engages the training he'd practiced in the DC10 simulator that corrects a bad bounce by powering up and going around for another landing attempt. We're now climbing back into the humid Maryland air. I am still expecting to crash, but flight recorders record a business-like conversation between the pilot and the control tower: "8535 heavy declaring an emergency go-around."

At 2000 feet and we are just below the cloud cover.

My back hurts and most passengers are nursing bruises and scrapes. Near the forward lavatory, a flight attendant's jump seat has separated from the bulkhead and she is helped to a passenger seat where she copes with the pain of compressed vertebrae. Still, she may also feel lucky, as she knows this kind of bouncing is the eminent sign of a crash.

In the seat behind me, a woman who'd spent the flight flirtatiously sharing the details of her failed marriage with her single seatmate launches into a litany of "Oh my God. Oh, my God!" This time, no one voices the obligatory apology I often hear, like, "Uh, sorry, chaplain. Didn't see you there." Maybe they've heard me swear too, and maybe they realize that sometimes swearing is a prayer.

When a passenger reports the smell of smoke, and the flight attendant passes him a fire extinguisher. A call from the tower explains that the plane has a blown tire and the smoky odor is coming from a smoldering tire through the landing gear bay. The remainder of its rubbery remnant is spread across our former runway. "Call out the trucks if you would," is the pilot's disembodied request to the tower. At 4000 feet, the pilot levels off and uses the public address system as if he's sharing the obvious. "Uh, I suppose you've noticed that wasn't how we like to land a plane, so we've called for a little assistance. The crew will be giving you some instructions for an emergency landing."

Inside my head, I lodge a protest. I don't want to back down there. Up here, it can be as if the crash never happened. Here in the lofty clouds all can be forgiven.

My head goes back to the goodbye speech given by our base commander, Brigadier General Brian Bishop. The general was an honest-to-god action hero, a former USAF Thunderbird Pilot whose likeness was used by Hasbro toys to produce a $29.95 chiseled, blonde-haired "Leader Action Figure." From a lit podium, he funneled his deep-throated words down an echoing microphone and offered his usual hype about our 332nd Air Expeditionary Wing being the most forward-deployed Air Force wing. With phrases like "fit to fight," and "cutting edge of the sword," he worked hard to tie his closing words to our heritage with the Tuskegee Airmen in World War II. Remember, he concluded, "You can count the days or make the days count!"

Now, here in the plane, I'm wondering how to make this moment count. Because this cabin has now become my war. My war is to keep sane. My war is to keep from thinking about myself and to pray for those the pilot would call "168 souls on board." There are muffled voices around me as if people are discussing what we should scream. No one wants to be first to cry, but clearly no one wants to die without protest.

Around me I hear some conversation among Air Force passengers concerning the aircraft structural integrity. We don't know it now, but the plane is unfit to fly. I fret that we might share the fate of the 256 soldiers who were on a DC-8 flying home from a Mideast deployment on Dec. 12, 1985. They refueled in Gander, Newfoundland, and crashed only 900 feet after take off. All souls lost. That was the year I submitted my paperwork to become an Air Force chaplain.

In chaplain school the next year, we were told the story of Chaplain Troy Carter who was only on that flight because he'd given up his seat to a fellow chaplain the week prior. Was Carter where he was supposed to be on that day? Was I supposed to be here now? What would the headlines say about our 168 people? Would they say I'd been a good husband and dad? Or would they remember the times I'd been absent, both physically and spiritually? My shortcomings had me feeling like I was being weighed on a scale in a spiritual assay office. The Man in the one-piece eyeglass is squinting at the life I had put down. I'd come to Iraq wondering what to tell people who were dying. I'd questioned what my role would be in facing death with the soldier. Now I have the luxury of asking myself, *What is it that I need to hear?* Do I allow myself to be scared spitless? Do I sing Kum Ba Ya?

I wonder if I will find the courage of the famous four WWII chaplains on the USS Dorchester whose ship was hit by a fatal torpedo in 1942. Survivors said that as the ship sank, the chaplains could be seen standing arm in arm on the ship's keel, leading an interfaith service. In the most published quote of the tragedy, survivor John Ladd called it: "The finest thing I have seen or hope to see this side of heaven." Somewhere I must have figured that if we died, no one would know what I did, but if we lived, everyone would remember how I responded to this moment.

With this story in mind and with breath back in my lungs, I rest my forehead on the seatback. I try to pray to the accompaniment of a jet engine, but I wonder, *whom should I pray? For myself? For others? Do I/we deserve to live more than those who flew home before us in coffins?* Around the cabin, people are praying, holding hands and even hiding their eyes by looking at their feet. I finally look around to see a single young officer wiping her tears. I lean forward and stretch my hand across the aisle to join hers. I find that it reminds me of the soft touch of my wife's hand. For both our sakes I want to hold it longer, but I am strained with the awkward angle I've assumed, so I break loose and join her hand with the chaplain assistant sitting beside her. I spend the next few minutes taking deep breaths in the Buddhist style of contemplation, but praying to the God I knew as a child. I ask God, "What about all these people?" A soldier was about to meet his new son for the first time. An airman is trying to make a marriage work again. They all wanted another chance today. "Will they have it?"

As we come in for the second attempt to land, and for what we all feel will obviously be our final attempt, the flight attendants tell us to grab our ankles and lower our heads. Soon they are yelling in unison, "Brace, Brace, Brace." They continue the chant so long that it is what most of us will remember as the worst part. Seconds before touchdown, the pilot gives the command to "brace for impact!" But instead of impact, we landed as smoothly as if suspended from a cable. In comparison to the first attempt, this landing makes no sense. None of it makes sense. The airplane is a total loss. Its main spar, the structural member that supports the wings while the plane is grounded, is broken. The plane should never have left the ground the first time, and the wings should have fallen off the second time.

Slowly, people look up from their crash/prayer position and start clapping. This is no contrived award ceremony. We dodge a bullet on this flight line just as Luis had on the Balad flight line. Suddenly his award doesn't seem that insignificant. We are awarded another day of life, and we gladly clap and clap like we never expected another tomorrow.

We are home and I realize what I must do now.

CHAPTER 13

THE ZAX PROBLEM

Private First Class Raymond Costa's prayer for God to forgive the insurgents that killed his battle buddy was the most spiritually heroic and spiritually haunting thing I've ever heard. For months after I returned home, the haunting was so bad that you might have thought I'd stooped to conversing with the dead.

I'm not talking about séances, though; I'm talking about how I was resurrecting issues and hurts that should have been dead and gone – most notably a 10-year-old disagreement with a chaplain colleague. It was like I was playing the role of medium – constantly resurrecting issues that should have been laid to rest.

I was not healthy; those thoughts were not healthy. In fact, my resentments toward this coworker plunged into a yearlong bout of clinical depression in 1999. Sometimes it was so deep that I was unable to do the simplest tasks, such as drive a car or order fast food. The depression became worse in the summer of 2000, the same year that Russia lost a submarine in the Barents Sea.

The Kursk, a nuclear-powered cruise missile submarine, sank with all hands lost. Some of her sailors survived six hours, waiting in a dark compartment and praying for rescue. In those final hours, they penned some desperate messages – prayers written in a doublespeak that both held out hope for rescue and hoped that their end would be mercifully swift.

My depression felt like that. It gripped my soul and left me feeling like the men in that boat — believing the whole time in rescue, yet shivering with hopelessness. My fright became not so much about dying as it was about the terrifying thought that this existence – this despair – would be what living would always be.

I spent most of the Y2K year sinking, flirting with old issues that I couldn't release. At times, these hurts spoke nearly as clearly as an audible voice, and one day my wife overheard me conversing in our walk-in closet with the disembodied spirits of hurt.

She decided she had heard enough, and she insisted I call my pastor. But whom does a pastor call? It was clear to her, and to me, that I should call my father-in-law, Wil Nuckolls.

Wil's 49 years in leadership of a single congregation had produced missionaries, pastors, chaplains, marriage counselors, musicians and, of course, his daughter. After an unexpected heart attack took my father in 1992, Wil sent me a sympathy letter saying, "I could never replace your dad, but I'm here to stand in his place wherever you'll allow."

Since then, I've considered him my "foster father." It is a decision I have never regretted, and it was the reason I called him on a November day in 2000 to ask for help.

His answer was to come to my house a week later with my mother-in-law in tow. He was 67, standing 5-foot-10 with a full head of hair that made him look 20 years younger. He led my wife and me into our living room, where we formed a circle of prayer. He read something he'd written just for the occasion, called, "A Litany for Our Deepest Hurts."

The litany was such a great help that I've shared it with many audiences over the past 10 years. No one has ever said that it was the magic pill they needed, but many have found it to be a strong first step toward deliberately ceasing to call the dead issues haunting their lives.

Leader: Because there are pains that do not heal as physical pain does with time, surgery or medication, we are engaged in this spiritual covenant in anticipation — now or soon — of eventual healing of our spirits.

Response: I accept and enter this covenant as if I were beginning a brand new journey in life.

Leader: The deeper the hurt, the longer the journey, whether in minutes, hours or days, to that healing destination brought about by forgiveness and release.

Response: I promise to move in that direction. I may not move as fast as you think I should, but today or daily I will release and surrender either all or some part of this cumbersome weight.

Leader: These hurts have many names such as bushwhacked, waylaid, back-stabbed, slandered, deceived, etc., and none hurts like that received from a perceived friend.

Response: I will cease giving it a name and simply reject anything in my mind and spirit that is counterproductive to what God has planned for me.

Leader: Ceasing to dwell on this matter is not a matter of weakness, for it will free your time and mind. Therefore, if you are willing to stop looking back and instead face a forward direction, then our mighty God will be better able to bless and direct a forward-moving life.

Response: Because I know you are right, I hereby give up to God my so-called "rights" I have attached to my hurts, knowing he will deal with those involved while also leading me "in the paths of righteousness for his name's sake."

With family and clinical help, I spent 10 years free of the debilitating depression I knew back in 2000. However, on the day of my Baltimore crash-landing, I realized that I wasn't fully recovered. I wasn't ready to die that day because there was something I still needed – something called forgiveness.

To find that forgiveness, God gave me a valuable roadmap in Raymond Costa's forgiveness prayer. Much like my father-in-law's litany, the merciful prayer contained a pathway to forgiveness. I decided I would take that path and journey toward both forgiving and letting go.

Days later, in the walk-in closet of my heart, I confessed that I had never really forgiven my former colleague. I had only replaced the depression with an elaborately resentful picture of the events. The events themselves were a combined matter of trivialities. During those days, my coworker probably would have told you that I spent the turn of the century being a selfish person. I would have told you that he had spent it being the most critical person I'd ever met.

The stubbornness we both held in our hearts became a real-life enactment of Dr. Seuss's, *The Zax*.

The Seuss story involves a North-going Zax and a South-going Zax who meet on a narrow trail through the Prairie of Prax. Both refuse to step aside to allow the other to pass. The Zaxes maintain their stubborn standoff until eventually a highway overpass is built around them. The story ends with the Zaxes standing "unbudged in their tracks."

I was the Southern Zax who was "unbudged" in my spiritual tracks. In my revised version, the other guy was the Northern Zax who was not only a stubborn fool, but also a big liar who was out to get me. He was paranoid. He was … blah, blah, blah – so went my amended view of history.

I was like a lawyer practicing for a big case, and I'd often rehearse my arguments in the shower, a walk-in closet or at a long stoplight. *Your honor,* began my imaginary argument, *these are trumped-up charges, the figment of a larger imagination. I submit to you* … honk, honk, from the driver behind me, and then it was back to the real world.

I'd done everything I knew to shake this larger-than-life ghost. I'd spoken to counselors, prayed with pastors and had my pastor (father-in-law) lead my family in a private forgiveness liturgy. I'd even written numerous confessional columns about forgiveness and depression that were thinly veiled attempts to resolve this "little" upset.

All along I knew, though, that the only way to exorcise this critical ghost was to confront my colleague. I always made excuses to avoid him: The upset was too personal for a phone call. The man lived too far away for a visit. You know the drill.

Finally, months after my crash-landing, I accepted a cross-country speaking tour that would bring me close enough to visit the chaplain. So after more than a decade of resentment, I mustered a small measure of the heroics I'd heard in the soldier's forgiveness prayer and broke my indignant silence. I emailed the chaplain with a meeting request.

Two weeks later, he graciously welcomed me into the church where he served as pastor. Inside his office, we shook hands and sat talking about the things important to everyone: faith, family and purpose. Gradually, the image I had created of him shrank — but in a good way. It shrunk to the size God made us all.

He told me that he had no memory of the details of those years past. Then he said what I needed to hear: "Whatever I did, I hope you will forgive me."

Then I heard myself saying the words I never thought I'd say: "I hope you will forgive me, too." And just like that, the resentment disintegrated, annihilated by grace, never to return.

There was no idealistic or dramatic ending; we simply shook hands and said our goodbyes. Yet we both found and bestowed the grace we needed. We were no longer Zaxes; we were fellow sojourners working out our salvation in this life.

Private Costa's prayer for forgiveness for his enemies, more than anything else, has taught me that if you want to avoid the path of a Zax, you might want to consider Jesus' advice when he said: "If a fellow believer hurts you, go and tell him — work it out between the two of you. If he listens, you've made a friend." While time may heal all things, I think the tone of Jesus' words favors sooner more than later, and He definitely would not approve of waiting a decade.

As Costa's prayer continues to teach me, forgiveness will always lead you down the hero's highway.

Made in the USA
Middletown, DE
04 October 2022

11670626R00076